Oh, My
GOSH

I OVER **SLEPT!**

FOREWORD BY JACQUELINE BOLLINGER, Ph.D

Oh, My
GOSH
I OVER SLEPT!

A Guide to Living Life On Time

AUTHOR AND MOTIVATIONAL SPEAKER
RITA D. ANDERSON

iUniverse, Inc.
Bloomington

OH, MY GOSH I OVER SLEPT!
A Guide to Living Life on Time

iUniverse books may be ordered through booksellers or by contacting:

iUniverse
1663 Liberty Drive
Bloomington, IN 47403
www.iuniverse.com
1-800-Authors (1-800-288-4677)

*All Scripture is in the Amplified version unless otherwise noted

ISBN: 978-1-4697-5137-5 (sc)
ISBN: 978-1-4697-5147-4 (ebk)

Printed in the United States of America

iUniverse rev. date: 02/08/2012

TABLE OF CONTENTS

"Set the alarm for the first day of the rest of your life."

-Your Personal Alarm

To every over sleeper—Tomorrow is waiting!

To "Dad & Kimmy"—I now realize that this experience was bigger than me! Thanks for calling me Daughter.

To Papa (pronounced Paw-Paw)—Thank you for changing my life with a much needed lecture!

ACKNOWLEDGEMENTS

The greatest part of who I am and who I must become is attributed to God! I would be remised if I did not claim the very reason for my existence . . . God. He is the only reason I am able to awaken from a night's rest, in my right frame of mind and therefore I give Him not only honor but all the glory which is the least that I can do.

Grandma, Auntie, Mommy, Snug, Beam

You all mean the world to me! Without you I would not be where I am. I am proud to call you "Gram", Mothers, Sister "Ma Soeur", Brother (best-friend), and most of all—my Family! I will love you always!

Godfamily

You showed me how to live well. You inspire me and make me want to achieve more than I ever have. You have always exposed me to the best in life. I love you all and thank you for being great role-models.

Pastor Q

Not enough $100 words in the world to sum up my appreciation for who you are to me—EVERYTHING.

Vel

The first person I told about the book being published and the only person who knows all of me. Our 14 years have been filled with ups and downs but we are still here! From our matching tattoos, to our matching trials and tribulations—it doesn't get any more connected than that. You are my bestie-sister, and I couldn't image this moment without you.

Love,
"Your Conscience"

Tally

My #1 Fan! You are the epitome of a (best) friend. You have seen me at my worst and remained true and for that I love you!

"The Fam" (Huey, JP, Joe-nathanT, Keke)

We've shared our triumphs and our tragedies! I thank God for the love and bond that we have! It's our time!

Staci

"The Great Encourager"! Even motivators have motivators—Thanks for being one of mine!

Dr. Bollinger

Not only have you been a cheerleader and a great influence in my life, but you have become my personal alarm. I can't tell you enough how much of a precious gem you are. I could speak for entire millenniums and still not be able to express how priceless your impact has been on me. Thank you for taking time to acknowledge and encourage me to pursue my purpose. I honor you for the gift that you are and I look forward to many great writings of yours in the future—it's your turn!

Daddy-Pie

As I said in High School, I thank God that I could call you father and friend. Daddy, you always mirrored what it meant to change the world and impact the lives of many; a legacy that I intend to continue and pass on to your "Grands" for generations to come. This is just the first of many impactful moments, and I hope that you are proud!

FOREWORD

My alarm began ringing in February 2011. Sherita Anderson had been my student the previous semester, and forwarded this manuscript to me for feedback. Having already come to respect both her mind and her spirit, I was honored by the request. Within a few hours I'd printed out the pages; by the end of that day I'd read every word.

This was not the first unpublished manuscript I'd read. Certainly other students, former students, colleagues and friends had shared their writing with me over the years: novels, memoirs, self-help books, and poetry. It is the first of these manuscripts that I could not put down until I had consumed the entire text, as if it were a personal call that I could not ignore.

Ms. Anderson knew nothing of my personal circumstances. She sought my advice as a writing professor, but my response to her dealt with the content of the text as well as the style and structure. She woke me up that day.

Her message is not her own, but a modernization of the basic concept of living a vibrant spiritual life. By framing this in the extended metaphor of using the alarm clock without "hitting the snooze bar" she takes a serious issue and presents it with an immediacy and humanity that can draw in anyone, from the sincerely devout to the doubters and seekers.

The narrative structure of this work is unique, a blend of a conversational voice with practical advice and well-integrated biblical references. She speaks with what I would term passionate compassion, as she urges the reader to awake, to avoid the temptation of spiritual lethargy, to greet the morning of our lives with strength and energy that can only come from God's will and presence in our lives.

The chapters are easy-to-read, and the concepts made simple and direct. Any reader, whether well-versed in the Old and New Testament, or unfamiliar with the Bible, will be able to comprehend the main points, and implement the suggestions. Having a strong spiritual background I found her biblical quotes aptly applied, not misread or misrepresented.

When I finished reading I almost immediately contacted her with encouragement to move forward with this project: edit, revise, publish. What she had to say needs to be heard by so many people, to be read by them. And this is a book that should be kept as a reference and reminder, to be re-read whenever this worldly existence lulls us into lethargy.

Sherita Anderson gave me a gift that February day. She shared her intelligence and her spirituality with me, and allowed me to encourage her to offer this gift to the greater population, a readership in need of such a text. As you continue reading this, accept each word as a gift that will strengthen and empower you.

Jacqueline A. Bollinger, Ph.D.
Erie Community College

STOP!
THIS IS YOUR ALARM SPEAKING

Good Morning! Let me begin our journey together with a little open confession. The morning I was to begin writing this book I actually overslept. Although this was not planned, it was certainly no coincidence. If you are reading this book right now then that means that I did not miss my appointment. My desire is to assist you so that you don't miss yours.

Can you imagine waking up to your clock radio saying *Besides this you know what [a critical] hour this is, how it is high time now for you to wake up out of your sleep (rouse to reality). For salvation (final deliverance) is nearer to us now than when we first believed (adhered to, trusted in, and relied on Christ the Messiah)* Rom. 13:11(AMP)? Now that's an alarm that commands attention. It never ceases to amaze me how often we ignore the simple nudges and tugs that we feel. Those inclinations that attempt to signal us when life becomes the status quo. We were created to be more and every time we try to fly below the radar our spirit becomes unsettled. It is imperative that you realize that your alarm is sounding off.

Okay so let's face it, we've all done it! We have all at one point or another overslept. Even if it is only a minute passed the time you normally wake up—you have still fallen prey to sleep's soothing clutch. So it's harmless right? WRONG! You couldn't be more wrong. The dangers of oversleeping are absolutely real and undeniably harmful. Don't believe me? Then why not ask yourself? What can I accomplish when I am asleep? Who can I help if I am asleep? How many times have I missed important appointments behind oversleeping? Still don't believe it's dangerous to oversleep? Take a moment to consider what it cost *you* when you overslept. The answer to these questions may shock you and possibly be more than you bargained for.

However, I urge you to consider this book as more than just another self-help book. Allow this book to become as valuable to you, as if you have just received a check for one million dollars. You see, this is an investment into your life, family, ministry assignment, and yes even your business. It is up to you to deposit this information into the bank of your mind and spirit.

You're probably wondering what on earth made me write a book on oversleeping? Well to be honest I was tired of having a life full of regret. At 23, I was sick of the life I was living. Why you ask? Because I wasn't living; I found myself sleeping away my days and not wanting to see any tomorrows. I wasted an entire year and 10 months heartbroken and discouraged waiting for God to honor my request and let me just get to heaven so that I wouldn't have to deal with my disappointing life anymore. *It wasn't until I was thoroughly disgusted with life that I was ready to do something different.* Believe it or not that is exactly how I came to wake up.

The truth is that this book is partially the result of a conversation that I was having with one of my best friends. The topic of that particular conversation was "Is This It?" Is this all that my life is going to amount to? What happened to the prophecies and promises that God allowed anointed men and women to speak into my life? Did they lie . . . or just mistakenly speak a message intended for another? Did they hear from God at all?

Had I missed the time frame wherein I was to receive the things that God had spoken? None of these panicked assumptions were the case at all. Although I had given up on every dream and every God inspired word spoken to me, it took God who created the original blueprint for my life to awaken me from a several yearlong nap. I hadn't missed God or my divine assignment but I *was* about to. That is why I now encourage you to digest this book and not merely read it.

To assist you in connecting yourself with your divine appointment I have allotted some intermittent spaces for you to *insert your name*. I have also added a few exercises for you to complete throughout the book. Please don't let the thought of a few spaces and two or more small exercises deter you from journeying to the life that you know you should be living.

Just think, we read magazine articles on how to get the guy, girl or money we want in the amount of time we want or what the latest celebrity gossip is, but when it comes to making a sound investment into our life we seem to hesitate if the hint of effort is implied. Trust me it's not a workbook. It's a catalyst for a better life; the one God always intended for you to live. Have you ever wondered why you are stuck in a rut? Why you haven't reached your full potential? Or why you can't seem to enjoy life? You might see an answer surface as you turn the pages of this book.

It is my sincere prayer to see people awaken to the urgency of the time that we are living in. The time for the hum drum status quo life is over. God wants us to live an abundant life. According to John 10:9-10, *I am the door: by me if any man enter in, he shall be saved, and shall go in and out, and find pasture. The thief cometh to steal, kill and to destroy; I am come that they might have life, and that they might have it more abundantly.* The "they" that The Scriptures were referencing are God's children. He came that *we* might have *life*. How can we then just barely exist in a regret filled never-ending cycle of mediocrity?

I won't say that after you've read this book every problem you have will instantly be solved. Nor am I suggesting, that the morning after you finish the last sentence of this book that you'll wake up with every great dream, prophecy or word of knowledge spoken over you manifested. But I can assure you that after you have read this and have taken principles and applied them to your life, you will begin to see change. Are you ready to redeem the time? It's as simple as setting the alarm.

PART I

THE SCENARIOS

1

LATE TO WORK

MONDAY,

". . . And that's today's weather forecast brought to you by The Tire Store and the Totally Gospel Morning Show. Good Morning! Everybody it is now 11am in the Queen city. Thank you for tuning in . . ." Jolted awake by one phrase "It is now 11am in the Queen City." you are now sitting straight up in your bed. Panicked you turn off the alarm and jump out of bed and rush to the bathroom all while repeating "11am . . . 11am . . . 11am!!!!"

"Oh, my gosh I overslept! I can't believe this. How could I have overslept? I set the alarm, but now I'm late!" Your shift started at 9am. Frantically you hustle to get ready and it is now 11:30am. Your ride has arrived and you're off to work. You just started this job; you can't afford to be late. You are definitely going to have to explain this to your boss.

As *you* arrive to work you hear "You're late. May I see *you* in my office for a moment?" "Oh No! What if I get written up? What if he docs my pay? What if I get fired?" Your heart and mind are competing in an unending race as you slowly take a seat. ". . . Others were depending on *you* to have your paper work completed so that they could set up appointments with our clients. We run a very organized company here and this sort of thing is highly frowned upon. Now because you are new I will let you off the hook with a warning, but this cannot under any circumstance happen again."

Throughout the day you are overwhelmed with constant feelings of uneasiness. You have a day's worth of tasks with less time to complete them due to your late start. "Awe man, I'm going to have to work through lunch to make up for lost time." No sooner than the words escape from your lips, your coworkers appear.

"Hey, *you* wanna go out to lunch with a bunch of us?" You know you have a deadline but you're hungry now. Besides it is only lunch. "Sure I'll go out with you all."

Lunch was great but good grief look at all those files! You only have three more hours and that is hardly enough time to even scratch the surface of your buried desk. Your phone won't quit ringing, and the clients are in rare form with their non-stop complaints. You're not making any progress so you decide to wait until tomorrow to tackle the rest of the heap. Exhausted you are finally able to clock out for the day.

"Thank God! Oh punch clock I am so glad to see you! I am so ready to get out of here; aren't you guys?" "YES! Hey, there's a movie coming out tonight did *you* wanna go and check it out with me and a friend of mine?" "What time does the show start?" "10:30pm!!! I have work in the morning." "Come on, It's only a movie, you'll be home in time to get enough rest for tomorrow. Just come on, it'll be fun! I'll call you when I'm on my way to your house."

TUESDAY,

". . . And that's today's traffic report brought to you by Big Lou's Burger Hut and the Light Radio Show. The time is now 10:15am in the Queen city . . ." Jarred awake by an all too familiar experience, you are knocking over everything trying to reach for the phone. "Hello USX Inc." "Hey Jen, can you put me through to HR?" "Hello USX Inc. How may I help you?" "Hello . . . AHEM . . . Hello this is **{Insert your name here}**. I won't be able to make it in today. I am sick. I'll try and make it in tomorrow." "Okay I'll let your supervisor know." "Thank you. Good Bye."

You hate the fact that you had to lie because you overslept. Especially since you knew that you shouldn't have gone to the movies last night. You manage to brush off the guilty feelings. After all, you'll go to work tomorrow and everything will be just fine.

WEDNESDAY,

"Do you have the Jones file?" "Um let me check . . . I know it's here somewhere. Oh here it is, but I haven't added all of the latest paperwork. I was going to do it today." "I told *you* last week that the file needed to be processed by Monday and since *you* weren't here I got an extension until today." "I'm sorry. I really am and I'll have it by lunch okay?" "Don't bother, I'll do it myself. I don't have time to wait. I was really counting on *you* to have this done—*ON TIME*!!!"

You've really messed up. You knew that file had to be in today but you kept acting as if you had all the time in the world. Work keeps piling up on you. You are struggling to keep your head above water.

"Attention all USX employees; there will be performance evaluations starting tomorrow. Please note that all employees with the last names beginning with the letters "A through L" have been scheduled first. When you punch out please be sure to find your name for your evaluation appointment time." Your heart drops as the announcement resounds in the office. The last time they did evaluations they were handing out pink slips. You can't afford to get fired. What will you do about your bills? "God please don't allow me get a poor evaluation. PLEASE!"

THURSDAY,

". . . Good Morning! Queen City! Thank You for waking up to the Morning Praise Party. Happy Thursday to ya, I hope you enjoyed that song by Kirk Franklin. It is now 8am in this beautiful city . . ." *You* have to be on time because today is evaluation day.

"Lord I know that you gave me favor on my job and I'm asking you please let my boss give me a good review even though I don't deserve it and please don't let me get fired in Jesus' name amen."

"Follow me please; Mr. Ross will see *you* now." "Thank you." You are a ball of nerves as you are escorted into your boss's office. "*You've* been here for 3 months now and I've got to be honest with you; you have had some rough moments along the way. I have here in front of me a total of 21 absences in the last two months alone. You have been written up one too many times, and you arrive late an average of twice a week. This is unacceptable. This company's success is reliant on the timeliness and efficiency of its employees. The reason for today's evaluation is to determine whether or not you qualify for an increase in pay. After examining your file I am going to deny the raise and recommend that a follow up evaluation be done in approximately one month. Do you have any comments concerning what I have addressed today?"

"Mr. Ross, I just want to say that I will do my best to change so that I can contribute to the success of this company. I apologize for not giving USX 100% of my abilities and you can rest assured that I will exemplify extraordinary dedication to the standards of this company."

"Very well then, if that is all, I look forward to our next meeting and I expect to see a tremendous amount of change in you."

"Thank you Sir."

Now you can breathe easy. The fear of having to go straight to the unemployment office after that meeting has finally subsided. Relieved you head back to work considering ways to change your bad habits. You hope to improve your performance in order to stay employed.

2

TEMPTATION'S LULLABY

December 6, 2007

It's a beautiful morning. You awaken to the sun shining over mountains of pristine white glistening snow, and the ruckus of your alarm sounding. Except for one thing, your clock—radio hasn't gone off yet. This pit of your stomach feeling wrestles you awake. You're not hungry but your gut is doing somersaults. For a few moments you lay pondering this situation with your eyes closed.

Your mind wanders back to a conversation you had the night before. "{Insert your name here} I told you that Temptation moved back here right? Just moved back and lives about an hour and a half away." The last time you saw Temptation things had gotten pretty intense. You try to regain your composure enough to respond.

"Are you serious?" "Yeah {Insert your name here}, I just had a conversation with Tempt not too long ago." You can't help but feel a little curious. With almost every fiber of your being you want to pick up the phone and call Temptation. You can't stop thinking about your last encounter.

It was July 22, 2005, around 7pm your cellphone rang. "Hello?" "Hello, this is Temptation. I'm going to be late but I am on my way." At around 9pm your cellphone rang again. "Hello?" "Hey it's me Tempt, I'm outside." "Okay I'll be right down." You opened the door to see Tempt looking good and smelling intoxicating. "Well, Hello {Insert your name here}." The mention of your name never sounded more amazing. "Come on in Tempt. We were just about to finish eating and play some cards." Walking into your crowded apartment, you introduced Temptation to the other guests. "Hey guys, this is Tempt. Tempt that's my cousin Mark, my friend Samantha, and my friend Veronica. Oh and those are Veronica's kids." "Hi everyone, it's nice to meet you all." "Hey Tempt, you hungry?" "Not too hungry but I could eat a little something."

On that note, you made your way into the kitchen with Tempt following behind. Lingering in a familiar tone, "**{Insert your name here}**, did you miss me?" Wantonly you answered. "Yes . . . I did." Overwhelmed by your emotions, you continue preparing the plate while trying to ignore the torturous conflict raging within.

Time was well spent and it was about 11:30pm. Everyone was sluggishly loafing around and naturally one by one they all cleared out—well not everyone. As the last person shuffled out of the apartment with sleep filled eyes they notice that Temptation was comfortably on the couch staring at the TV.

"Uh **{Insert your name here}**, aren't you going to tell Tempt it's time to go?" "Well Tempt came late . . ." "Uh huh ok. You should tell Tempt to leave it's getting late." "Tempt will only stay a few more minutes and lower your voice! Goodnight." "Goodnight."

Returning to the couch where Tempt was, you seated yourself on the opposite end. The room took on an awkward hush. "You're awfully quiet over there." With that, Temptation stretched out to the full length of the couch; causing Tempt's head to strategically rest in your lap. After a few flustered moments Tempt leaves the room. When Tempt returns arms extended you assume the posture to mean that Temptation was leaving. Falsely relieved you embraced Temptation.

The embrace turned into a shower of severely impaired judgment. You'd crossed so many lines that you didn't know how to get Temptation to leave without ruining your relationship.

"Um, Wait . . . Wait!"

"What?"

Through heavy rapid breaths you continue. "I can't do this—I gotta stop." Temptation was laughing but not stopping. Minutes rolled by and at that point the small shower quickly turned into a category 5 hurricane, with Temptation telling you that everything was fine. You were so caught up that you no longer resisted. With your guard completely shattered you submitted to Tempt's subtle assault.

Finally you open your eyes. "How could Tempt be back?" You contemplate whether or not to call your familiar friend. "I can't call Tempt. We haven't spoken in over a year. But it's only a phone call, it can't hurt.

I could just call and say 'Hi'. We don't have to meet up or anything. It'll be good to hear Tempt's voice." You are fighting a serious battle and you haven't even gotten out of bed yet.

"NO . . . NO! I AM NOT CALLING TEMPTATION! I know God told me to leave Temptation alone and I can't keep going around in circles like this. I'm so close to my destiny that I can taste it. Just when I thought that I was doing fine; I find out that Temptation is back and closer than ever. Oh God! Please help me!"

A Second Look

Perhaps you think that the scenarios are different. If you do, then you are mistaken. There is no difference between them at all. You might be saying to yourself right now, *What does the fight between my flesh and my spirit man have to do with oversleeping?"* The answers lie in the not so evident details you may have overlooked while reading.

In situation one, you plugged yourself into a scene where you actually overslept. You simply didn't hear the alarm. As long as you could justify your actions to yourself you kept repeating the cycle of oversleeping. Until the evidence became tangible and a drastic change was necessary, you allowed yourself to take for granted each day. In doing so, you jeopardized your job and your future with a slam of the alarm.

In situation two, you found yourself convinced that you had a few more minutes to spend listening to Temptation's Lullaby. You entertained one bad choice after another. You were willing to risk it all for a moment of fleeting pleasure. Much like a baby being nurtured, you were soothed to sleep by the gentle seducing whispers of "everything is fine" and "it can't hurt to call". These thoughts or statements were used to make you comfortable enough to doze off, justifying the "innocence" of the event turned trap. This however, is not your mother's sweet voice crooning songs of love and comfort. Listening to this lullaby kept you playing a risky game of spiritual 'Russian Roulette'.

When you or I become so relaxed in a potentially harmful or hazardous situation it is as if we have overslept. We hear the alarm sounding but now due to poor judgment we are late for work, have missed an important appointment or are stuck in an endless cycle of yielding to temptation that leads us to spiritual death.

The most prominent characteristic of oversleeping is that it is sneaky. No one ever plans to oversleep, but it certainly doesn't just happen either. That statement probably seems a little contradictory but believe me it's not. So, how can something be sneaky and at the same time not just happen? Let's explore this question for a moment.

The Thief

A thief sneaks into a house undetected. He rummages through personal belongings and prized possessions, then leaves unnoticed. You return to a ravaged house. Did the thief accidentally rob you? No. He watched you. He waited for an exact moment. He knew what he wanted and how to get it. All of the steps he took resulted in your house being robbed. It wasn't by any means an accident. Likewise, when you overslept there were actions that took place first.

There is an exercise that I want you to do. Go and grab a plain piece of paper and an ink pen. Write out your daily routine. This is not a 'Things to do list' so don't start out writing for example; 1.) Brush teeth, 2.) Wash face, etc.

Instead I want you to start by writing the time that your alarm is set for. The next day, write down the time that you started your day and left for work. Then write down the time you arrived home and the time you started preparing for bed. Please be honest. Don't make estimations on the time(s) that I have asked you to record. You are going to need to be able to take this sheet of paper with you. I suggest you purchase a little note pad if you don't already have one.

If you do this exercise correctly you should have results that resemble the following:

Tonight I set the alarm for { : } tomorrow morning.

Tonight I went to bed at { : } am/pm.

Today I woke up at { : } am/pm.

I left for work at { : } am/pm.

I got to work at { : } am/pm.

I got home from work at { : } am/pm.

I got ready for bed at { : } am/pm.

I set the alarm for { : } tomorrow morning.

Take a look at the sheet once you've completed it. Are you waking up and starting your day on time? If you are CONGRATULATIONS! You can close the book right here. If not then I have a few questions. Are you hitting the snooze bar before you finally drag yourself out of bed? Is the time that you set the alarm different from the time you actually get out of the bed?

By completing this exercise hopefully you have become more aware of the fact that although you are setting the alarm, it is possible that you may also be taking the appropriate measures to successfully oversleep.

My challenge to you is to try this exercise again. Only this time I want you to track your actions over the course of a week. This will allow you to see a more accurate display of habits both good and bad that you possess as it relates to time. We'll further journey in this thought later on in the book.

PART II

THE PANIC ATTACK

I have both said and heard it said "It's not my fault I overslept." Well in the panic attack that only lasts a split second—the blinders come off. The truth now stares us dead in the face and there is no place to hide.

This is the moment of truth for you. You have just realized that you have made a colossal mistake, one that could possibly have grave consequences. In this period of time it is impossible for you to lie to yourself. You can't ignore the fact that you messed up big time. Or can you?

As if lightening has just struck you, your heart is racing and your mind is bombarded with what seems like and armored tank full of questions. Sudden bursts of regret and fear alternate causing you to momentarily hyperventilate. You manage to pull yourself together. For the next 10 minutes you try and do what would normally take anywhere from 40 minutes to an hour to complete. You are now in the throes of a panic attack. But you aren't alone; there are many others experiencing the same scenario.

"And he came thither unto a cave, and lodged there; and behold, the word of the Lord came to him, What doest thou here…?" 1 Kings 19:9 (KJV)

3

GRANNY'S STORY

"Granny what's wrong?"

"Nothing's wrong baby."

"Then why do you look so sad?"

With tear filled eyes Granny manages to utter, "I regret the way my life turned out. I used to go to church, and I know God had plans for my life. I thought that I could keep going to church, drink, gamble and shack with my man. I did that for years and now I'm old."

"Granny that doesn't mean it's over and you can't come back to God."

"Baby I've been praying. I just want to go back to how it used to be. You know back when I know His voice."

Granny knew she had wasted so much of her life and she knew she hadn't experienced His power in ages.

"Granny it's not enough to pray. You've got to be willing to quit living like your life is your own."

"I know baby but how could I have let time slip away like this?"

I would've never thought that granny would ever confide in me like this. Here I am 20 years old and a 72year old woman is telling me she has regrets. Shouldn't she be encouraging me?

Granny like many others after taking inventory of their lives felt overwhelming emotions of fear and regret. The alarm didn't start ringing when Granny confided that day. It had been ringing for years she just chose to ignore it. The day that Granny confided in me was what I call the **Panic Attack**. You may prefer to use the phrase "moment of clarity." Call it what you'd like but the bottom line is when the blinders come off truth is ultimately what you are faced with.

Granny's story has isn't far from your own. It's not an age thing. It's a lifestyle thing. Take a moment to gather inventory of your life. How's it looking? Are you where you need to be? Does your life right now mirror the full potential of your future? Or is it a catastrophe evolving into a lifetime of fear and regret?

So what do you do now? I'm glad you asked. Don't Settle! If the life God called you to live is not the one that is playing on the big screen at the moment, take time to find out why. Don't just sit there and settle for the way it is going. Don't live in the Panic Attack. Learn from it.

LIVING IN THE PANIC ATTACK

It is very dangerous to live in the Panic Attack. The second you see clearly you are immediately struck with a surge of fear. There are some people maybe even yourself who live in that surge of fear 24 hours a day, 7 days a week and 365 days a year. This is not a healthy way of living; in fact it's not living at all.

The Bible states in 2 Tim 1:7 *For God did not give us a spirit of timidity (of cowardice, of craven and cringing and fawning fear), but [He has given us a spirit] of power and of love and of calm and well-balanced mind and discipline and self-control.*

Fear is a crippling and debilitating emotion that if not handled properly can limit how far you will go. If you live in fear you become incapable of living the life God wants and intended for you.

Fear will cause you to settle in a place not designed for occupancy. Elijah was a prophet that infuriated Queen Jezebel to the point that she sought to take his life. He fled and under the intense pressure he prayed for God to take his life. Elijah still hadn't met Elisha during his stay in the cave. What would've happened to Elisha if Elijah had not come out of the cave when God called him? Elisha was supposed to receive the mantle of Elijah when he passed from this life to the next but how would he have obtained the position and authority if Elijah lived in the panic attack? **(1Kings 19; 2Kings 2)**

You can't allow fear to be the deciding factor in what do or how you live. You have entirely too much to accomplish and too many lives to impact to let fear or intimidation stop you. Don't hide in fear when you were made to stand in power. For it is the power that you live in that negates the fear that tries to attach itself to the seed of your Destiny. The only way to control fear is to not let fear control you.

A few years ago a favorite preacher of mine, Dr. Joyce Meyer spoke a message about doing whatever God called you to do even if you have to do it afraid. Although I understand what the point of the message was—it would later be challenged by the voice of God speaking expressly to me.

God had impressed upon my heart that if I wanted to bring Him the glory He deserved I couldn't settle for life in fear. Why not bring Glory to God by doing what He said to do in power? Even though fulfilling purpose in fear can be a triumphant testimony, it is my belief that doing it in power is a stronger tale of triumph.

God has not given us the spirit of timidity or that of a coward but of miraculous power and of love and of a well-balanced mind. We owe it to God to walk out his plan in total confidence in spite of our failures.

So if your life is limited because of fear I want to give you an opportunity right now to talk to God. Read through this next statement before reading it aloud. I don't just want you to repeat something you read. I want you to know what it states first. If you truly subscribe to it and come into agreement you can declare it aloud. Are you ready?

Lord, teach me how to get out of fear and grow into a power filled life. Your desire God is for me to have fullness of life according to your word. So even though I mess up big time, I need you Lord to forgive me, order my steps and help me get back on track In Jesus' name. Amen.

If you have just prayed this prayer then you are now well on your way to waking up on time.

PART III

SETTING THE ALARM

4

THE NIGHT BEFORE

"Baby, why are you running late today?"

"I was so exhausted last night that I forgot to set my alarm." Last night was so much fun I was out with my friends and I got to see that new movie. It was great.

"It's not like I oversleep that often. I mean I do have an alarm clock."

"What's the point in having an alarm clock if you don't set it?"

There are several things wrong with this scenario. First, the mindset of the over-sleeper is often where oversleeping occurs. What makes this a bad situation is that the over-sleeper feels justified in occasionally oversleeping.

Secondly, the over-sleeper sacrifices priority in order to have temporary pleasure. Having fun last night and being caught up on all the latest happenings took precedence over taking the appropriate actions that were necessary to yield a good and fruitful tomorrow. Thirdly, the over-sleeper fails to set necessary boundaries and therefore has become a careless steward of valuable time.

On my way to work *late* after having overslept, I was involved in what came to be a life changing conversation. My grandfather, while driving me to work for the umphteenth time due to lateness started to ask me questions. He looked over at me and said "Rita tell me what you did last night." Of course being in no mood for the lecture to come I rattled off some of the nights occurrences. His first response wasn't as bad as I thought it would've been.

"Rita." He said in his gentlest stern voice. "You are doing too much." I assumed he was going to stop there because I said "Well Papa, I have a lot to do and everything is important. So I guess I just have to learn how to spread it out a little better." Why oh why did I say that? I thought that the lecture was over and if it was that last remark caused part two.

"Rita, your oversleeping didn't happen because you missed your alarm."

"What do you mean Papa?"

"Your oversleeping today started with what you did last night. If you had gone to bed at a decent hour, you would have been rested enough to be up on time today."

I was 20 then and didn't really put a whole lot of thought into what grandpa had said. Instead like most 20 year olds, I kissed him on the cheek and blew off his comments all while thanking him for the ride. My problem was that I didn't value time. Over the years however, I have learned that if you don't value time you will waste it.

Do you know the difference between spending time and wasting time? To spend time is to invest one's energy on a goal, plan or individual(s) in order to produce a permanent, positive and meaningful outcome. To waste time is to carelessly squander energy on doing things that don't produce anything other than maintaining one's present state. So how do you figure out the type of steward you are with your time? Take a few minutes to complete the chart below. Doing so will assist you in determining your current usage of time. I suggest that you take an average Friday to record your actions accurately; as some of the items tend to take place on a weekend.

Spend	Time (HPD)	Waste	Time (HPD)
Devotions/Church Service		Phone(gossip)	
Family		Computer Games	
Education/Business		Television	
Dating/Friends		Sleeping in	
Spouse/Fiancée		Retail Therapy	
Exercising		Procrastinating	
Hobbies/Recreation		Social Networks	
Total Hours		**Total Hours**	

*Key: HPD = Hours per Day.
        1.00 = 1 hour
        .50 = 30minutes
        .25 = 15 minutes

If more than an hour use the same method i.e. 2.00 = 2 hrs, 2.25 = 2hrs and 15min. Remember be honest. The only one reading this is you.

After you have calculated a typical Friday, take note of the results. Are you shocked by what you have just read? Multiply the results by 52. Is your life headed for a panic attack? Although these are just examples of how one can spend and waste time. I am sure you can figure in a few other ways that I may have missed.

Too much time wasted is just as bad as not enough time spent. Don't think that just because you have higher numbers on the "spend" side that you are in the clear. What you are in need of is balance. The trick is finding the "Happy Medium". You know the place where you can have a fun and exciting life while taking care of business. That is the life we all seek but seldom attain. You're waiting for me to tell you how. Don't worry I will.

"We sacrifice purpose for pleasure and wonder why we stagnate in life."

5

SEVERELY IMPAIRED VISION

Let's explore one of Grandpa's comments from our story for a moment. He said "Oversleeping didn't start with you not hearing the alarm. It started the night before." What does your "night before" look like? Are you accepting the current state as the way it will always be? Are you listening to the "If I were you(s)"?

What if David's night before scenario was like yours? What if he was accepting Saul's armor as the only way to have victory over Goliath? In 1 Samuel the 17th chapter the Bible depicts a story of a young shepherd boy that kills a giant. I have heard this story told a million times over and have read it a few times myself. What grasps my attention are the 38th and 39th verse in this chapter; (1 Samuel 17:38-39 NKJV)

> So Saul clothed David with his armor, and he put a bronze helmet on his head; he also clothed him with a coat of mail. David fastened his sword to his armor and tried to walk, for he had not tested them. And David said to Saul, "I cannot walk with these, for I have not tested them." So David took them off.

With all of Saul's armor David was severely impaired. I can imagine Saul's helmet was probably fit for the likes of Shaquille O'Neal. I further imagine that David was about the size of Steven Q. Urkel. Can you picture Shaq taking off a helmet and putting it on Urkel's head? Now that is a truly hysterical sight to see right?

I believe that is how ridiculous David looked with Saul's armor on. I also believe this is how crazy you and I appear to God weighed down with all of our wrong ways of doing things.

A helmet protects your head right? In David's case however, the oversized helmet most likely severely impaired his vision. Why place something over your head that won't protect it? If he was going to fight with that helmet he might as well have fought blind folded. Stupid idea you say? Don't go throwing stones just yet. We allow ourselves to become visually impaired for the sake of others and self. How? I'm glad you asked. Every time you make a decision based on the opinions and or reactions of others you become visually impaired. You are now in fact wearing someone else's "helmet" in other words their mindset.

Others' opinions of you are the limitations that they have set for themselves. Once you come into agreement and accept their opinion as truth, you invite them to dress you for war.

War! What war Rita? Believe me there is a war. There may not be any guns, knives, swords or boulders but there is definitely a battle. Not only do you have to fight with the "Giant" but at the same time you are fighting clad with the limitations of others. If the "Giant" doesn't get you, the limitations are sure not to stop until you are dead. Oh and If that's not a war I don't know what is.

It is not until you strip down the armor of fear and possible persecution that you truly have victory. If anyone were to ask me when I thought David won the battle against Goliath, I would say "It was when he said no."

Are you wearing someone else's helmet? If you are hoping what worked for 'so and so' will work for you, then lie down and get ready to die. If you are being led by the popular vote of friends and loved ones, then start planning your funeral now. The only opinion that matters is the one God has concerning you. Am I telling you to avoid sound counsel? No! You need that. All I'm saying is how can you listen to the "Girl If I were you" and the "Man if it were me" before you heed God's gentle unction warning you not to go there or do that? The bottom line is 'Quiesha and thems' opinion is not going to matter when you are toe to toe with your giant.

I stated earlier that we become visually impaired for the sake of ourselves, allow me to clarify this portion of the statement. We act on impulse instead of following God's voice. We sacrifice purpose for pleasure and wonder why we stagnate in life. We often avoid the uncomfortable in desperate attempts to escape rejection. We no longer stand for what we believe in. Instead we close our mouths and turn a blind eye. We run with the popular opinion of the day and unfortunately set ourselves up to fail.

Believe it or not you and I are in a lifelong battle with a very real enemy. If he can keep you bogged down with fear or going in a continuous cycle of sin he wins. The enemy desires to sift us as wheat (just like he wanted to do to Simon Peter) according to Luke 22:31-32 NKJV, *"And the Lord said, "Simon, Simon! Indeed, Satan has asked for you, that he may sift you as wheat."*

Let's define sifting. It is Satan's very desire to pull us apart. He wants to break us down into nothing more than a light dusting. He does not have our best interest at heart. He's only out to prove that God messed up in creating us.

Since this is the case the helmet we choose is important. We have two options. We can have a mindset that tells us not to ruffle any feathers, just go with the flow. Or we can have a mindset that tells us God doesn't lose and be determined to live the life He said we can.

Satan knows that once you learn from the panic attack and change accordingly he loses. He believes it so much that he continuously tries to create distractions and smoke screens, so that you either forget to set the alarm or you ignore it all together when it does sound off.

Setting the alarm is all about making adequate choices necessary to live the abundant life God designed for you. Refusing to make these choices will cause you to waste time, live in the panic attack, settle for the worst possible life, and live chained to the ideologies of people who didn't create you.

Do you value time? Make the choice to set the alarm. Change your mindset and your behavior. This is the beginning of obtaining a balanced life. Live the rest of your life not consumed by worry, fear, doubt and regret. It's not too late for a mindset change. It's the right time right now.

"Do you really have a few more minutes?"

6

THE SNOOZE BAR SYNDROME

"I can see clearly now . . . Happy Tuesday everyone . . ." With sleep filled eyes and sluggish limbs you reach over to your night stand. With all the strength that you can muster you slap the snooze bar. Why, just so that 5 minutes later you can do it again? I never understood why anyone would go through all that trouble in order to lie in bed for a few more minutes.

I, myself am guilty of another more heinous form of the snooze bar syndrome. I would actually set my alarm for 45 minutes earlier than I wanted to get up. So that when the alarm sounded I could wake up, reset the alarm and continue to sleep. I really thought that this was smart. After all, I wasn't hitting the snooze bar. It still really wasn't worth all the unnecessary commotion.

A few years ago I experienced the worst case of snooze bar syndrome I had ever come across. I lived in a quaint little apartment with my sibling. One morning before I was ready to awaken, I heard the annoying buzzing of an alarm clock. Being that the walls were paper thin in our humble abode, I immediately knew the noise was emanating from my sibling's room. A few minutes drone on with this irritating buzzing and then silence. This continues 28 times in a one hour period. Later that day I am still disturbed by the mornings' occurrence, and I decide to ask my sibling some questions.

"Why did you set your alarm?"

"I needed to get up on time. I had to go somewhere."

"Then why didn't you get up the first time you heard the alarm?"

"I hit the snooze bar."

"I know as a matter of fact you hit the snooze bar 28 times in an hour."

"Really?"

"Really."

"Next time could you just set the alarm for when you actually want to get up?"

Does this conversation remind you of anyone? Let's say that it does. You wake up every morning after slamming your snooze bar multiple times. You roll out of bed, shower quickly and race to the kitchen. You grab whatever your definition of breakfast is so that you can run out of the house in enough time to make the 5 minute grace period at work before you are considered late. Sound about right? Of course it does because everyone who has snooze bar syndrome lives like this.

So what is snooze bar syndrome? I define it as **the inability to adhere to warning signs; using a conscious or subconscious thought in order to maintain a level of comfort, or familiarity.** For example, a situation where you are tempted presents itself. While walking through the mall one day you spot a pair of beautifully crafted Louis Vuitton Sunglasses. You know that they cost about $150 dollars and you also know that your phone bill is due this Sunday. The temptation to buy the glasses is almost too much to bear. You really want these glasses and they are on sale. Just as you pick them up you feel convicted.

"Put the glasses down. You can't afford them right now." There it is again. That still small voice that always seems to appear when you are bordering on potentially unfavorable territory. But what the heck you can borrow money from someone for your phone bill. You've purchased the glasses anyway and now you can't find anyone who will loan you the money. Had you listened to the still voice your phone would not have been turned-off.

This is a very mild instance, but there may be an instance that is stronger in your own personal life. Perhaps one that has had or will have more grave consequences if you ignore the warning signs. Can you really afford to hit the snooze bar one more time? The life that you want deserves the best you living it. Your life is waiting for the individual who does not accept the convenience of having a snooze bar and definitely does not oversleep.

Setting the alarm only works if you don't ignore it when it sounds, it's a two part process. You have to set the alarm and wake up. There are consequences that come along with enjoying those "extra five minutes". Your life may be all the proof you need of that.

Excuses we make in the aftermath

"It's not my fault I overslept."

We are all guilty of using this statement (or one very similar) to shun the responsibility of our actions. The problem with this is that we actually believe it. We have convinced or shall I say *"convenienced"* ourselves into thinking that we hold no part in the misfortune of oversleeping. It is precisely that type of reasoning that keeps us from truly enjoying life.

"I thought I had a few more minutes."

This being yet another of the many statements of convenience we offer up to justify ourselves. How is it that "It's not your fault" if you "Thought you had a few more minutes"? The truth is that it is our fault. All too often we have taken for granted that time was on our side. In fact, we've wasted so much of it that all we have left now is a lifetime full of regret.

Think of it this way, a few more minutes in a burning house and you die. A few more minutes in an abusive relationship and you risk severe injuries and possible death. A few more minutes in a 'dead end' job and you are headed for a serious bout with depression. Do you really have a few more minutes? Are a few more minutes all it takes for you to finally wake up? Or is that just something you keep telling yourself, because somewhere along the way, even though it is a horrible situation you are somewhat comfortable?

The alarm of your life is sounding and you hear it. You're just not ready to get up yet. You still don't value time and why should you? That's what the snooze bar is for right? You know that one great excuse you have not to follow your dream. The "I can do it tomorrow." or "Maybe later." How about "I just need one more (Minute, Hour, Day, Week, Month, Year)?

We all have our own case of "Snooze Bar Syndrome". At some point the snooze bar syndrome reaches a level of intensity and we are "Jarred awake by an all too familiar experience." But why wait until the alarm is sounding off so loudly that you can't stand it? By this time you are all out of sorts and you no longer have the energy that you once had. Now are you ready to get up?

"Don't you think it's time to change your reach?"

7

DESTROYING THE SNOOZE BAR

There is nothing more that I wanted to do that day, than to destroy my sibling's alarm clock with a larger than life sized mallet. It would've made me feel a lot better. I mean it wasn't like it was being used properly anyway. I wonder if this is how God looks at us when we offer up excuse after excuse about how or why we can't do what He said we could.

I am reminded of Moses' case of Snooze Bar Syndrome. Moses is oversleeping and clinging to his insecurities. Despite the fact that God intended to use him flaws and all; Moses hits the snooze bar and sleeps on. He makes the statement to God (as if He didn't already know) that he had a speech impediment. We find this in Exodus 4:10-13.

> And Moses said to the Lord, O Lord, I am not eloquent or a man of words, neither before nor since You have spoken to Your servant; for I am slow of speech and have a heavy and awkward tongue. And the Lord said to him, Who has made man's mouth? Or who makes the dumb, or the deaf, or the seeing, or the blind? Is it not I, the Lord? Now therefore go, and I will be with your mouth and will teach you what you shall say. And he said, Oh, my Lord, I pray You, send by the hand of [some other] whom You will [send].

Moses was comfortable as long as he didn't have to speak. The moment God said "I want you to go", Moses is quick to offer excuses. God is getting pretty upset with Moses' protests by the 14th verse.

> Then the anger of the Lord blazed against Moses; He said, Is there not Aaron your brother, the Levite? I know he can speak

well. Also, he is coming out to meet you, and when he sees you, he will be overjoyed. You must speak to him and put the words in his mouth; and I will be with your mouth and with his mouth and will teach you what you shall do. He shall speak for you to the people, acting as a mouthpiece for you, and you shall be as God to him. Ex 4:14-16

*Quick Bible Study Note—Verse 16 does not mean that Moses is going to be like God in the sense that Moses will take the place of God. Rather the correct interpretation of the latter part of this verse is that Moses will act as a translator for God instead of God speaking directly to Aaron.

God was angry with Moses because His original intent was to use Moses despite the fact that he stuttered and stammered. Snooze Bar Syndrome made Moses miss his miraculous healing. If he had only learned to destroy the snooze bar, He might have been able to tell Pharaoh himself what God had spoken.

Destroying the Snooze bar isn't easy. We have over the years become accustomed to the routine fumbling to reach the nightstand. Although destroying the snooze bar may not be easy, it is definitely necessary. Since we don't have an "ACME ACRES" sized mallet to take care of the snooze bar, we must first redirect our reach.

Out of habit we reach for excuses to stay in the "same ol', same ol'." If you and I can practice reaching for reasons to do a thing instead of reaching for the reasons we can't, we will be well on our way to successfully destroying our snooze bar.

Try it now. Grab a pen and paper and write down one excuse that you have been using for a while. Be completely honest you are the only one who is going to see it. Now instead of justifying why you can't, I want you to write on that same sheet of paper what you are going to do because that excuse doesn't exist anymore.

For example, here is my excuse: I can't write a best seller because I don't have money to publish it on my own. Now the fact that I didn't have the money when I had a dream of writing a book (that could possibly later become a best seller), had absolutely nothing to do with my ability to actually write the book. The excuse was just my way of hitting the snooze bar. I changed my reach from grabbing a comfortable excuse to grasping a concept that if I write it the money will come.

The second task that we need to perform is to live life like there is no snooze bar. What would you do if your alarm didn't come with a snooze bar? You would most likely wake up the first time it sounded. Make the decision today that there are no more excuses to fall back on and no more minutes to waste.

Take a look at David's story again (1Samuel 17:38-39). He told Saul that he couldn't wear his armor and took it off. The end of the story was that he won against Goliath. Two things happened here. First, He said "NO". It takes a very strong person to say no when everyone else is saying "Yes". Second, He took off the armor. He wasn't afraid to shed something that didn't belong to him. Whose limits are you not saying no to? What opinion are you too afraid to shed? What excuse are you pushing the play button on every time you consider doing something different?

You have been living like this for too long and freedom is one decision away. You can either be like David, and kill your Giants or you can be like Moses and stay stuttering. No excuse is worth losing out on the miracles, joy and fulfillment that God intends for you to have. It starts with you not accepting and justifying The Snooze Bar Syndrome.

I was a person who constantly sought approval. I didn't even realize that this in and of itself was a case of the Snooze Bar Syndrome. I found myself after a while feeling very empty and frustrated. I wasn't living life I merely existed. As a teenager I tried my hardest to make sure that I was in on the latest happenings of who broke up with whom (typical teenaged stuff). As an adult at times I flew beneath the radar because I cared what people would think about me. Don't get me wrong I didn't care about everything others thought just what they thought concerning certain things in my life.

I was trapped by the opinion of others and the limits that I accepted as my own. I was about 18 years old and standing outside of my church's annual Tent Revival waiting for it to start. While waiting a woman (who later would become a good friend of mine) told me that there was quite a buzz generated about me. At this time I was fresh out of high school and beginning to embrace my call into ministry. My Father in the Gospel, The late Bishop Nathan S. Halton, had advised me to join the Ministerial Alliance and placed me on the Altar Worker's Team. I was active with youth ministry and had even begun having detailed dreams where I would be preaching. However, nothing could've prepared me for what she was about to disclose.

She went on to inform me that there were some women (much older, 40 something year olds) that didn't believe that I should be working in ministry. They made such comments like "who does she think she is?" and "I wonder why Bishop let her do that, she ain't nobody?"

This woman didn't stop at telling me what they had to say concerning me. She ended the conversation by saying "That's what I like about you, Girl you don't care about people's opinions. Just keep going the way God is leading you." I eventually heard the snickering and snide remarks first hand. I went through an array of emotions. First, I was angry then I was hurt. After that I was indignant, and lastly I was accepting. I had processed through anger and pain while continuing to work the Altar and participate in Minister's meetings. But in the back of my mind I kept hearing those snide remarks. It wasn't too long before I washed my hands of the entire notion that God had called me to serve in this capacity.

After all, these were predominant people in our church that didn't approve of me. How could they be wrong? And with "Saul's" armor I attempted to go. I wanted to be in ministry with the approval of everyone and the majority cheering me on. When that didn't happen, I buried my purpose in a cemetery called rejection. I wasn't able to shed off the limitations that those women dressed me in.

I slowly eased into the background and anytime God would sound the alarm to tell me to wake up, I would hit the snooze bar. "But God I can't go." **SLAM!** "They don't want me to speak." **WHAM!** "I don't think you can use me." **BAM!** It would take years for me to destroy the snooze bar. God allowed me to hit rock bottom and then he sent word that he approved of me.

You see, fear and doubt had me comfortably oversleeping. I thought of every excuse possible to stay asleep. When all God wanted was for me to accept His approval as all I would ever need. God wants you to know that no matter who doesn't agree with the design, He has the last say, because he created you. You are the perfect vessel for what He has purposed.

PART IV

WHEN LEADERS OVERSLEEP

Depending on an over-sleeper

Read Matthew 26:36-45(AMP)

We as leaders have a responsibility to those whom we serve. In the passage on the previous page we see the story surrounding Jesus' prayer in the Garden of Gethsemane. Here Jesus takes Peter, James and John to accompany him in his journey.

The only task they had was to pray and keep watch for Him as He goes and speaks to God. Jesus returns three times to find His disciples sleeping. Even though they knew Him as the Messiah they failed to realize the importance of not oversleeping. There is nothing worse than depending on someone that has overslept.

The responsibility that we as leaders have is to first be dependable. Those that follow you whether it is a sibling, a friend, a child, a congregation, or a company, they have to be able to depend and rely on you. From your timeliness to your advice, dependability is an essential characteristic of a great leader.

8

A CAN LABELED PEACHES

I was extremely hungry one day, and I had a craving for something sweet. I didn't want Lucky Charms™ Cereal or a Peanut Butter and Jelly sandwich. Nope. What I wanted was a nice big bowl of chilled peaches from the can. I rummaged through my cabinets and retrieved a bowl, the can opener, and the last can of peaches. The anticipation of satisfying my craving was building at a rapid pace. I took the hand held can opener and I began to open my can of peaches. I finally get the can opened and empty its contents into my bowl.

As I am pouring the fruit into the bowl however, I realize that it's not peaches I'm pouring out. "PEARS!" How could it be pears? "Did I open the wrong can?" I grabbed the can and examined it. "No, It says right here, Peach halves in heavy syrup." So how come I'm eating Pears? Someone was sleeping on the job. But I'm the one who was left disappointed. I was depending on the employee who packaged the fruit to deliver the right contents into the appropriate container. Likewise, the person that seeks your advice and example of how they should conduct themselves are counting on you. They need you to lead them and not just look like a leader.

I would have to guesstimate that about 95% of leading is non-verbal. That leaves the other 5% to be what actually comes out of your mouth. I stated a moment ago that people are counting on you to lead them and not just have the aesthetics of a leader. I wouldn't want to follow someone who constantly dodged responsibility and offered up excuses for why they weren't able to complete a task but had an executive title, a corner office with a cushy chair and a nice view. Would you? Of course not because you know that it takes more than that to qualify as a leader.

How can you lead if you aren't able to resist the comfort zone? I believe that there is a certain level in leadership where an individual begins to hit the snooze bar. The person has attained notoriety and a pretty sturdy pedestal. They have 3 cars, 2 houses, a beautiful family and a successful career. There is nothing wrong with being blessed with the finer things in life. I only question the value placed on leading once the "desired wealth" has been acquired.

What happens when leading conflicts with the comfort levels of that leader? What happens when that pedestal isn't so sturdy? For most, it is at this time that they hit the snooze bar. They become so acclimated to the accolades and loyalty of those around them that they gain comfort and sacrifice conviction.

The drawbacks of this are that they lose integrity. They say more and mean less (they are talkin' loud and sayin' nothing, that's what the old folks used to say). They become more concerned with self-preservation and maintaining the level of comfort. Part of being a leader though, requires one's knowledge of the fact that leading is not going to be about self.

Early on in the course of ministry God showed me a vision. One night while I was at the church I attended, the youth decided to gather and pray as we often did. God led me to take a seat in the choir's section of the pulpit. I had been in prayer for a while and then as I was speaking to God I opened my eyes. I saw the side of the church that I was facing full of people. These people seemed to be in various positions. Some postured with their hands raised while others sat staring at me.

Then the Lord spoke to me "Do you see these people?" and I not knowing why I was seeing these images very bewildered answered "Yes Lord." He said "These are all of the people who will die if you don't do what I've called you to do, and their blood will be on your hands." Talk about responsibility. I was only a teenager. Why was God talking to me? Even back then God wanted me to know that in spite of how I tried I would never be able to escape who I was.

It wasn't until about 6 years later that I had a confirming conversation with a dear friend. Being that I was at a major cross point in my life, I was in no mood to revisit past visions. I had gotten used to the comfort of living in my excuses. I found myself second guessing everything in my life.

My calling became distant and blurry. My life became chaotic and noisy. I was hearing everyone else's voice but God's. I wanted to walk away from everyone including God. Would you believe that just as I arrived at this point in my life the alarm sounded again? As I reached for the snooze bar one more time, God intervened.

It was July 4th, 2008. I was invited to attend a barbecue at the home of my "Big Brother and Sister." I arrived with the intention to leave an hour after I showed up. God had other plans. While there a friend with whom I'd shared struggles and debated excuses with, began to engage me in a conversation that started me back on the path to my purpose. She began speaking about how God kept bringing me into her mind and spirit. Normally I would have totally blown off anyone who spoke of God calling me. However, the statements that she made were dead-on and although I am stubborn I couldn't ignore her words.

I had never heard such a plea. "Sherita I need you to be healed enough so that you can begin to heal others. I need you to be in your position so that I can move on to what I have to do, and unless you are positioned I can't get what I need from you which will hinder my growth." Was I hearing correctly? Was this one of those persons I had seen in my vision come to life? Here she was pleading with me to wake up and get back into alignment with purpose and destiny. What she needed, the information, tools, prayer or advice that I had to give, she couldn't get if I was asleep.

It was awful convenient for me to oversleep. The longer I avoided and ignored God calling me, the more time I had to enjoy the comfort of rebellion. I spent the next 6 years in a constant cycle of rebellion. I purposefully tried to contradict everything that God had ever allowed anyone to tell me about my call to the Kingdom. Why? Because I was not yet aware of the fact that being called to lead was not about me. I was so focused on protecting myself from the pain of rejection that I had encountered when I first accepted the call that I chose to run, hide and fight.

Eventually the comfort of rebellion wore off. That's when my life started spiraling out of control. I battled with depression and thoughts of suicide. I wanted to die. I wasn't happy or joyful. I wasn't fulfilled. I just merely existed.

Life had gotten so bad that I can remember one morning waking up (after crying throughout the night) asking God why He let me wake up after I had begged Him to take me in my sleep. Thank God that He doesn't answer all off our prayers.

If it wasn't for this divine 4th of July appointment (that I almost didn't attend), I would've probably never awakened to the fact that there are people waiting for the gifts, talents and words yet to be spoken that are inside of me.

Who am I to deny someone the opportunity to be healed, delivered and set free or even blessed? I can hear my spiritual father now saying "I have a Charge to keep and a God to Glorify." This too is my motto as I journey along the path before me and act unselfishly in my purpose.

Is your assignment begging you to wake up? You may not want to ignore the alarm this time. Who's to say that you have five more minutes? I'd like to share the story of Jonah. For the next few moments I want you to suspend your basic Sunday School knowledge of Jonah. When this story is told often there is much attention given to the whale that swallowed Jonah. Allow me to show you Jonah's story in a different light. **Read Jonah the 1st-4th chapter** just to refresh your mind about the story. God tells Jonah to preach to a city that hated Israel. Jonah not wanting to see evil people spared runs to escape the assignment. While Jonah is fleeing from the Will of God, He gets tired and falls asleep. Yep you've guessed it that is where we drop anchor (No pun intended. Okay maybe just a little bit). Jonah 1:5,

> Then the mariners were afraid, and each man cried to his god; and they cast the goods that were in the ship into the sea to lighten it for them. But Jonah had gone down into the inner part of the ship and had lain down and was fast asleep.

Jonah convinced himself that it was okay to go to sleep. He got comfortable even though he was running and trying to hide from God. By the next verse Jonah's assignment is begging him to awaken. Jonah 1:6,

> So the captain came and said to him, What do you mean, you sleeper? Arise, call upon your God! Perhaps your God will give a thought to us so that we shall not perish.

God sends a storm, and the crew on the ship is a frantic mess. Jonah's actions were endangering everyone he came in contact with on that ship. Who is in danger of dying (spiritually, emotionally, and/or mentally) because you are asleep and comfortably out of your appropriate position? The storm's purpose was not to harm any of the ship's crew. The storm was an alarm sent by the hand of God to wake Jonah up. Ignoring the assignment in your life means that you are willing to assume responsibility for the spiritual, mental and emotional death of hundreds, thousands and possibly countless others. Are you willing to have blood on your hands?

So who exactly is depending on you? For Jonah it was the shipmates and Ninevah. In Jonah 1:8-11,

> Then they said to him, Tell us, we pray you, on whose account has this evil come upon us? What is your occupation? Where did you come from? And what is your country and nationality? And he said to them, I am a Hebrew, and I [reverently] fear and worship the Lord, the God of heaven, Who made the sea and the dry land. Then the men were exceedingly afraid and said to him, What is this that you have done? For the men knew that he fled from being in the presence of the Lord [as His prophet and servant], because he had told them. Then thoy said to him, What shall we do to you, that the sea may subside and be calm for us? For the sea became more and more [violently] tempestuous.

The shipmates ask Jonah what they should do. If Jonah had been like some of us he would've said "keep rowing so you're in pain, we're almost there." The Bible states Jonah knew the storm was a result of him not following God's instructions. He also knew that the only way to calm the storm was to get off of the boat. If someone is following you, they are expecting you to have their best interest at heart. Earlier I suggested that 5% of being a leader is verbal. If this is true then you must agree that words carry immense weight.

Every word that you utter could be the death, life or deliverance of a person. As a leader you cannot afford to have your best interest at heart. I believe that Jonah knew the weight of his words and didn't want to risk the lives of those around him. He instructs them to throw him over board (Jonah 1:12)

What? Why did Jonah instruct them to throw him over board? I'm glad you asked. Jonah was a real leader. He accepted responsibility for his actions. He had others best interest at heart and he did not abuse the power of his words.

Although it may possibly be 5%, the verbal portion of leadership should never be minimized. There should never be an ulterior motive behind the instructions that you give. Ulterior motive and hidden agendas are indeed the character traits of being Pears in a can labeled Peaches. You'll say or do what sounds good and benefits you but the people following you will be left disappointed every time.

Jonah's story is far from over. In the 3rd chapter, Jonah hears the alarm again. He has made it out of the Whale's belly and onto dry land. God tells him a second time to go to Ninevah. Only this time instead of running away he makes the journey to fulfill his assignment. It is my belief that the assignment would've kept resurfacing. Jonah's life as a fugitive from the Will of God would've grown increasingly harder. He would've never escaped who God created him to be. If he had died at any time during the course of his run, he would've died with the "label" of a leader and the blood of the lives that God intended to save on his hands.

The reason that God told Jonah to go to Ninevah a second time was because his word never changed. Since God's word hasn't changed concerning who we are, we have to ask ourselves "who will die if I don't stay in or return to my proper place?" We need to, as my sibling's Sunday school teacher once worded it "count up the cost." We need to gain a firm understanding of what it takes to lead.

9

THE UGLY SIDE OF LEADING

January 16th, 1816,

"Captain, gather your troops. Today is the day that we conquer our enemy."

"Yes sir."

"Troops today we forge on to victory. Break down your campsites and leave no trace of occupancy."

"Sir, excuse me."

"Yes private."

"Sir the weather is below freezing with zero visibility. How will we know that we are going toward the enemy's camp?"

"Captain."

"Yes sir."

"Suit up."

"Yes sir. Troops wait here until I return."

With that having been said the captain sets out to obey his orders. Minutes turn into hours and hours turn into days with no word from the Captain. Through the piercing cold temperatures and the white out conditions the fearless leader makes the trek toward enemy lines. The soldiers confidently await the return of their commanding officer.

About three days after the Captain disappeared into the never ending veil of snow, a soldier spots a figure barely moving in the distance. As soldier's set up a line of defense they notice that the figure seemed to be waving something at them. They watched only to realize that it was their Captain.

Some of the soldiers ran out to assist their leader. "Captain what was it that you were waving at us?" "I was waving a map that I drew up. A map that will lead us so close to our enemy that by the time they figure out what's going on, we will have destroyed them all."

"Captain, what happened to your leg?" "When I left the temperature was dropping rapidly. Along the way my gear became less resistant to the relentless elements. As a result I've gotten severe frostbite and can hardly move my leg." The troops were discouraged at the news of their leader's misfortune. "But sir, we need you to show us which way to go." "I can't go with you my injuries are too great. Here take the map, follow it carefully. I have left markers throughout the path. Go and remember Today is the day that we conquer our enemy."

I have heard it often said by another of my former Bishops', that "Leaders don't come first, they go first." I understand this statement to mean that as a leader you and I get the "honor" of making the first set of tracks in a snowy blizzard. It is up to us to travel in white out conditions, in order to draw up a "map" that will guide others safely through the tough times. Even if it means we return "frostbitten".

The ugly side of leading is the side that is seldom talked about. People don't acknowledge this side of leading because no one wants to subject themselves to pain. Despite what hype there is concerning the leadership role, the truth remains that sometimes leading hurts and it most definitely costs.

To become a great leader you have to embrace the ugly side. So what is this ugly side? Quite simply, it starts with the development process. In the development process there is no lime light. So if you are called to be a leader and you are expecting an entourage from day one then this will be an "alarm" moment for you. The way God often develops leaders is by separating them from that which is both familiar and comfortable. For me this was one of the most painful transitions that I had ever experienced. I freaked out when one of my mentors told me that God said that I would never fit in. I was in shambles because like most, I wanted to be accepted. The more my friends dwindled, the more saddened I became.

After separation comes rejection. Rejection was almost as hard for me to handle as separation. At least when you were a part of the "gang" you knew that you were accepted. No one ever expects to be rejected by those that they are closest to. However, it is important you remember that they were close to who you were. They don't know who you are as a leader. They never expected you to leave the pack.

Once you have been separated from those who "knew" you and rejected by those you held in close regard, then you are in a place called loneliness. One day during the development process, you will look around and realize that you are all alone. Ever increasing in the awareness that, friends aren't calling you to hang out. All you have is loneliness, the painful indicator that makes a person cry out "Why me?" "What did I do to deserve this?" You may find yourself asking God to send you just one person that understands this whole process.

You see, the development process doesn't come with a disclaimer; so you probably won't know when it's approaching. It is easy to become frustrated in loneliness. You are going to question everything and wait for what will seem like an eternity for answers. God is still there, He just seems to be far away. It is in this time that your emotions will try to convince you that God is not with you and the He doesn't care for you. You cannot let your emotions lie to you. You aren't going to die of loneliness. It is just that God needs alone time to restructure you. He needs you not to be readily influenced by the "group mindset."

Before He separated you from the group of peers, parents and on lookers, If he had told you to go into business or ministry you would have consulted with the group. After separation has taken place, if He instructs you to lead or serve you only have Him to confer with. That's what God wants. He wants us to trust that His voice is the right one to follow. According to *John 10:27, The sheep that are My own hear and are listening to My voice; and I know them, and they follow Me.*

We have to recognize the voice of God. Following after what we feel is God is not the same as following Him. How can you follow if you don't know that it is Him that is speaking? This part of the process can be rather extensive depending upon how connected you are to the group mindset.

After you have endured all of this you must be ready to jump into your leadership role; right? Well, not exactly. You haven't been tested yet. Tested? Yes, even though you have endured all of this there is more. The testing for each of us will be as different as the thumbprint we all have. The objective however, is undoubtedly the same. The categories of the tests are in the areas of **Obedience, Trust, Faithfulness, Humility, Integrity and Character.** Each test is designed to either improve or impart. He improves the weak areas of our life and imparts instructions on how to access and utilize the tools that are needed to complete our purpose. God intends to equip us for the assignment. Therefore, God tests us so that the end result is that we are vessels that bring Him glory. So now that you have been separated, rejected, lonely, frustrated, emotional and tested, what's next? It's time to step up to the task of leading.

Just as an infant takes its first steps, you will wobble and teeter-totter a little bit and perhaps you may even fall down. Pretty soon though, you will have strengthened your legs and you will begin to gain confidence enough to keep going. There are going to be some bumps and bruises along the way, and thus continues the ugly side of leading.

The fact that you are a leader doesn't mean that you will automatically be exempt from pain, challenges, or setbacks. There will be people that won't agree with your every decision. Your job is not to convince them to agree with you but it is to guide them having their best interest at heart. How do you guide someone who doesn't agree with you? First, pray for wisdom concerning the matter. Ask God how you should handle the individual(s). If necessary, ask Him to change their disposition concerning this area from cynicism to trust.

If they still show no desire to follow, realize that you are not called to lead everyone to agree with you but you *are* called to lead. There will be those around you that only seek to gain status. These are the ones that want to be seen with you. They will pat you on the back and smile in your face when times are good. However, when times are bad these same individuals will be the first to talk about you and leave you to go down by yourself. It is hard to differentiate between those that are supportive and those that are only around to gain a bit of the spotlight. Usually it is time that will uncover who's who.

You will make mistakes. At any given time it is possible because you are human, that you will say or do something wrong. A mistake is not the end of the world. If you can correct it do so. If you cannot, seek God and those that it affected for forgiveness, take full responsibility for your actions. Ask God to help you to get through the trying time, work to rectify the situation and move forward.

The day that you hold leadership responsibilities and authority, no one hands you a cape. You do not become invincible, and you do not get special powers. This means you will have hurt feelings occasionally. You will still get aggravated. You will still have moments of discouragement, and disappointment. There will be moments that you will most definitely feel like giving up and throwing in the towel. As a matter of fact the minute you accept the role all of these things will intensify. It will almost be like you are walking around with an enormous bulls-eye painted on your back.

There is a misconception that leadership equals invincibility. Well allow me to dispel that myth right now. It doesn't. This misconception is the reason why potentially great leaders don't last. The way that I now see leadership is like this, Leaders are the first line of defense (kind of takes the glamour right out of it doesn't it?). If a leader loses his/her composure even in the slightest way that defense will surely break down.

Again I state, there will be times when you will want to walk away or crack under pressure. Due to the erroneous belief that you are somehow invincible, you will often times be forced to protect this image. You will have to put your best game face on through private upsets, tears, runny nose and all.

You can't show signs of distress to those that you lead every time you are upset, but you can present yourself as human. Don't try to have all the answers and appear to have it all together all of the time. Don't fall into the trap of playing a superhero. This is by no means an excuse to be an emotional tyrant. You can't have bad days every day. You can't act as if everyone else should suffer because you are suffering. Remember it's not about you. In the end, know that you don't have to wear a cape and solve all the problems of the world, the office or even the day.

Although leading is not synonymous with invincibility, it is synonymous with sacrifice. Sacrifice is a huge portion of the ugly side of leadership. Your life is no longer your own. You as a leader will be required to give sacrificially on a consistent basis. This means that the time you used to spend leisurely will almost become non-existent.

It also means that leading will now be your primary focus. You will not only be sacrificing time, energy, and self-interests but also personal comfort. There will be tough decisions to make and at times major risks to be taken. The bottom line is that it takes a lot to be a leader.

The ugly side of leading is the equivalent of the Captain in the story, risking frostbite. The captain knew that some sacrifice was inevitable in order to lead his troops to victory. To him the sacrifice was worth it because he believed that they could achieve victory. Even if you are with challenges and unfavorable conditions you are still called to lead.

In order to lead you need the ugly side of leadership. Jonah ran into the eye of a storm trying to outrun the ugly side. Moses forfeits his promised land trying to play superhero when he hit the rock instead of speaking to it **(Numbers 20:11).** It is indeed the ugly side that shapes, conditions and teaches us to hear God, pay attention to detail, maintain a good character and follow instruction.

Trying to survive leadership without having been properly processed is suicide and has grave consequences. When Moses thought he knew best he ended up missing the land that God had for him. When Jonah played his game of "hide and seek" he was found in the belly of a great fish. You will lose a lot more in the grand scheme of things if you try to escape the process.

Don't think that the glitz and glam is all there is to being a leader. It is easy to want to be a leader once you see the fancy cars and lavish homes but don't reduce leadership to having nice things. You need to be able to lead with the same integrity and character whether you live in the lap of luxury or a rundown 1 bedroom studio.

Leading is not contingent upon the cars you drive, home you live in or bank account you build. They are tangible blessings that God may choose to give a leader. The "stuff" is just a possible result of having been a good leader. Believe me there is an ugly side that every leader has endured before they came to the place that you see them in presently.

10

SLEEPING IN THE PULPIT

Recently I was invited to attend a service at a friend's church. While there the service seemed to last forever. It felt like midnight at about 8:30pm. I had a rather close seat to the pulpit and during the service I glanced up at the pulpit to see the Bishop of the Church drift deeper and deeper into a coma like sleep. This caused me to chuckle and glance around to see who else noticed what I had. The Bishop's seat, as most in traditional Pentecostal churches was facing the audience so I was absolutely sure that I wasn't the only one to witness this. Some had indeed taken note which was evident as they giggled and nudged their neighbor. Others had simply chosen to ignore it altogether.

Funny as it were this scene registered a more prominent issue within the Church as a whole. Not in terms of denomination, but rather as an entire body of believers. This however, is in no way, shape or form humorous.

It seems that the church now is the weakest it has ever been. Divorce rates have hit an all-time high, an increasing number of Pastors have become more concerned with building "Mega" churches than with building people and wannabe Prophets are "prophe-lying" houses and cars instead of casting out demons or relaying what God is speaking not just what he said yesteryear. Itinerant preachers are more concerned about receiving the highest honorariums than leading souls to deliverance, healing and salvation. What has happened to the Power that used to reside in the Body of Christ?

The Bible states in Matthew 5:13, *You are the salt of the earth, but if salt has lost its taste (its strength, its quality), how can its saltness be restored? It is not good for anything any longer but to be thrown out and trodden underfoot by men.*

God calls us salt. So why are we bland? The Kingdom of God is supposed to set the standard for the entire world. Instead we have taken on its attributes. The world does not need another "MEGA CHURCH". What the world needs is a Mega Kingdom. I want to go on record stating that I am not against any Bishop, Apostle, Pastor or Overseer of any thousand plus member church. With that being stated, that 15 or 30,000 seat edifice is about as good as the Kodak Theatre if no one leaves better than they came in.

Growing up I can remember preachers and church mothers saying "The Church is like a Hospital." A Hospital is a place where people go to receive healing. However, The Church now is more like the Hospital waiting room. It is a shame that people who need immediate spiritual care and healing are having trouble finding "Hospitals".

For the most part they that are severely broken and hurting are finding waiting rooms. A waiting room is a place where you sit anticipating a solution to what ails you. There are no Doctors in the waiting room and no healing process taking place there either.

Can you imagine going to a hospital that is full of waiting rooms? They have comfortable seating, beautiful amenities and no solutions. Yet, this is the exact setting that many in our churches are experiencing on a regular basis. If the Church is the Hospital, then the Pastor should be the Doctor. Doctors diagnose and offer possible solutions. Likewise, Pastors and Leadership should be equipped and ready to speak (pray, advise) to conditions of the body, spirit and soul, in order to guide people to Godly solutions.

The word Kingdom is used as more of a catchphrase than a goal. Do we really comprehend what it means to be a Kingdom? Understand that the Kingdom of God shouldn't be reduced to a flashy new building with state of the art equipment and a 10 acre parking lot with valet service. The focus needs to shift from building wealth to building well. You cannot build well without the proper foundation. This means that our foundation has to begin with the undeniable truth that God has commissioned us to impact people in every facet of their lives.

God is not concerned with how luxurious your establishment is, and hurting people don't care about how many seats you can fill in every service.

Both God and hurt individuals desire to see effective ministry. It is the effectiveness and functionality in ministry that makes us the Kingdom.

The enemy has waged an all-out attack on the Kingdom of God. His goal is to discredit and destroy the Kingdom and its impact. Since leaders are the first line of defense Satan tries to hit us the hardest. While we cannot pretend that we aren't wounded, now is not the time to tuck tail and hide. Instead we need to become the enemy's worst nightmare.

The enemy doesn't have a muzzle on the mouth of God, so we shouldn't be afraid to see what the devil is up to and stop him dead in his tracks. Wage war on the enemy's kingdom by preaching, teaching, discussing, counseling and praying aggressively about marriage, divorce, sexual immorality, salvation, sin, restoration, wisdom, stewardship, spiritual gifts/warfare etc.

People are tired of going to the Church of the waiting room. They have chronic cases that require immediate attention. They can't afford to sit in a waiting room anticipating a solution. They are expecting permanent change.

Referencing Matthew 5:13, ". . . *it is not good for anything any longer but to be thrown out and trodden underfoot by men."* We find that if we are not in the position to impact others, we are considered to be "good for nothing." I don't know about you but I personally do not want to be thought of in ministry as good for nothing. Good for nothing leaders breed good for nothing people who stay in good for nothing situations and live good for nothing lives. How long will you perpetuate this unrelenting cycle? How much longer do you think God will sit and watch you waste precious time?

In the latter part of verse 13 states *"but to be thrown down and trodden underfoot by men."* It is my firm conviction (based on but not limited to this scripture) that there will come a day in which God will become fed up with the ineffectiveness of those who hold leadership position and as a result he will replace them with people who have his heart and follow his direction.

I am calling all sleeping leaders into accountability. If you are leading in any capacity in your local assembly be sure that you are an active part of the solution and not a component that is useless and soon "trodden under foot" or discarded. Don't get caught sleeping in the "Pulpit."

"No amount of gain measures up to the solid investment
made into your family."

11

FAMILY MATTERS

"After 20 years of marriage I can't believe it's really over. What's worse is that my company is at the top of the 'Fortune 500' list and I have no one to celebrate with."

What a tragedy, no one thought this could ever happen to a couple like them. His wife of 20 years filed for divorce last week and he just got served today. They seemed happy together. Always smiling and holding hands like two love struck teenagers. What began as a fairy tale match made in heaven, ended as a nightmare on Stanbury Lane.

There was no infidelity and no signs of abuse. So what happened? Mr. Stanbury was an entrepreneur who made it big developing computer software. Mrs. Stanbury was a corporate lawyer who made Senior Partner at her Firm. They met at a social affair and after a yearlong courtship they decided to wed.

They never seemed to have a harsh word to say to each other. Shortly after their nuptials they learned that they were going to be parents. All seemed to be going well for them. They enjoyed their beautiful custom built home, luxury cars, not to mention their lavished bank accounts.

Looks can definitely be deceiving and in this case they most certainly are. Year 15, the Stanbury's have a 14yr. old son and are too tied up to notice that he is not doing his homework and is skipping classes. The days at the office are getting longer and longer. Time spent with Adam and each other is almost non-existent.

The family mealtime routine consists of Adam getting a text message that his food is in the microwave, while Mr. and Mrs. Stanbury are seated in the Family Room watching CNN eating in silence. No one knows how this routine got started but it seemed to be the beginning of the end.

Every award ceremony or social gathering that the two attended, they never let on to the distance growing between them. Yet now after 20 years the two are seated in a lawyer's office screaming at the top of their lungs, fighting over whom deserves the blame.

All the signs were there. The family had gradually become more and more preoccupied with their individual lives and they neglected each other. The husband had his business to run and the wife had immersed herself in her case load to keep her from coming face to face with her loneliness, leaving the son to fend for his self. But when in public they put on a great show of a picture perfect life that didn't exist. They didn't want to sacrifice the appearance of being happy to actually work at being happy.

One can only pretend for so long. Mrs. Stanbury finally had enough. Overworked and stressed out, at wits end with trying to figure out their son and not getting anywhere near a solution for her marriage, she filed for divorce. By the time they tried to fix the problem neither one of them knew where to start. Now like so many others, they have become a part of a growing epidemic.

The definition of what it means to be family has been twisted, stretched and selfishly reconstructed. For most a family meal resembles that of the Stanbury household. Nowadays, spouses are like strangers passing in the night and children are like hotel guests that need chauffeuring services. With the hustle and bustle of work, school, church (if attended), after school activities, sports, meetings and business trips, communication is almost obsolete.

It never ceases to amaze me that a text message or a "Post—It Note" tacked to the fridge can be used as a means to touch base with people who live in the same house. How is it that we have lost the ability to communicate? Whether you choose to accept it or not, lack of communication is the very reason why our youth are living double lives.

I went to a very diverse high school. There were all types of religious views, sexual influences and ethnic backgrounds. Due to the fact that our school was a very well-known institution with students who were the sons and daughters of Pastors, Lawyers, Doctors, Architects, City Officials and Entrepreneurs, we had to conform to an invisible standard of perfection that was a tremendous weight to bear.

The school pushed extremely hard on students to perform well above the norm and this was evident during freshmen orientation. By senior year most people knew what College or University they were going to and some had even been awarded with Scholarships. However, I had a schoolmate who applied to four Ivy-League Schools.

She was talking about how she wanted to go to these schools and how good her grades and SAT scores were. One day the guidance counselors called the seniors down by last name to line up and share with them our acceptance and rejection updates.

Many students were excited to share this information while others were disgruntled at the request. My schoolmate however, had not shown to school this particular day and everyone wondered where she was. It was later that day that we received word from a few other classmates that she'd been involved in a terrible car accident.

I believe it was said, that this girl's parents assumed that she was out with friends the night before and didn't realize that she hadn't returned all that evening. They hadn't become aware of her absence until they received word from the Hospital. As the story unfolded, we all later found out that the accident wasn't entirely an accident.

This girl was severely depressed because she didn't get Into any of her choices and she didn't want to tell her parents or anyone else. She drove herself Into a brick wall in hopes that she would die. She felt as if she had no hope and her parents had no clue that she was upset at all.

I stated prior to this example that lack of communication is the very reason why children are living double lives. As a parent your first priority is to tend to your child. You need to know what they are feeling and why. You also need to know who their friends are and what influences they've adopted as life guidelines.

What you ignore today can and will jeopardize your family's future. No amount of money or material gain can measure up to the time invested in building a strong foundation for your family.

It is imperative to the success of your lineage that you value the home life. Attention is the one thing that can't be supplemented for in a family. You are responsible for both setting the standard and value system that your child will need to produce a successful family of their own.

Refer to the chart that you completed in chapter 4. How much time do you spend with your family? How much time do you spend with your mate? Are you making a valiant effort to ensure that your family is solid? Is your relationship with your spouse/fiancée headed in the right direction? If not now is the time to shift into gear.

Make the appropriate adjustments so that the needs of your family (beyond financial) are met. You are not only shaping your family but you are creating an invisible guideline as to how your children's family and their children's family's will function.

PART V

REDEEMING THE TIME

12

WRONG PLACE, WRONG TIME

No matter age you are presently, you have undoubtedly wasted a portion of valuable time. I can make such a statement because you wouldn't be reading this book right now if you haven't. By the same token I wouldn't have written this if I hadn't. With that having been stated, allow me to become a little more transparent. I want to share with you a natural reflection of a very spiritual conflict.

"God show me what to do, I really need your help here . . . PLEASE!" I uttered these words as I walked my usual 20 minutes between a 2 bus commute to work. As if waiting for God to crack the sky, I listened for his voice but all I got was silence. "Come on God, talk to me . . . I need you." A few moments drone on as I am still walking, No make that gliding across the ice-kissed city streets. Still listening and hoping for an answer Nope . . . nothing, not a single whisper to be heard. It was then that I changed my focus from praying to reflect.

You see, a few nights prior to this I was a willing participant in what could only be described as a monumental waste of time. For the past nine months I had been in a convenient "friendship" with an acquaintance that I had known for quite some time.

I had convinced myself that this relationship was okay. After all friendship with him was harmless, and at least I would have someone to hang with when I felt lonely. About a month after we were entertaining each other, I noticed that he would engage me in conversation pertaining to us. These conversations centered on us becoming romantically involved with each other. He would state the level of attraction he felt towards me and the value he placed on the friendship.

The more we spent time together the more he began to suggest that I stay the night with him. I had always said no until one night I didn't. "Rita, um do you mind staying at my place tonight because I have to work early tomorrow?" Reluctantly I answered "um, I don't know?" It still wasn't a no and he knew it. "Well I mean it would be easier for me because it's already late and you can just stay at my house until I come home from work." "Okay, but I don't want to make this a habit alright."

All the way to his apartment I was wrestling with the idea that I had actually said yes. "You are compromising again Rita. You know you never stay at any male friend's house, it is one of your rules." This was not a statement of conscience. That was the Holy Spirit allowing me to realize that I was going the wrong way.

"It'll be okay, I'm not going to have sex with him. I'm just going to fall asleep next to him. I'm not even going to touch him, we're just friends." This wasn't the devil's doing, it was me trying to reason my way into being comfortable with bad judgment.

In all that reasoning I didn't take into account that he would touch me. So there I was lying in bed with a man that I wasn't married to. He pushed and tried every which way to see just how far he could get with me. He was asking questions of intimate nature while pulling me closer and closer towards him.

Although we did not have sex, we definitely crossed the lines of appropriate and inappropriate as it relates to just being friends. We eventually attempted to drift off to sleep. Amidst the constant noise of the unfamiliar apartment building, our coughing fits and the unpleasant snoring that was emanating from my 'friend'; I lay there thinking.

'Why am I here?' 'How come I can't get to sleep?' It became alarmingly apparent that God was not going to let me be comfortable in this situation. I begun tossing and turning, shaking and wrestling awake every five minutes with an increasing flood of questions inundating my mind. 'Is this really what I want?' 'Is this going to be worth it?' 'Why didn't I stick to my convictions?' 'What am I doing?'

6:45am finally rolls around and my "friend" as he is getting ready for work turns on the television and we exchange 'Good Mornings'. Then as if he had read my mind he says that he had a horrible night of tossing, turning and coughing. I in turn, say "I know. I had a rough night too." We laughed it off and then while attempting to ignore the alarms sounding off in my spirit; I ask him if he wanted me to stay put until he returned from work. To which he replied that it was up to me. I told him that I would probably go home after I tried to get some rest there first.

I did try to get rest after he left but every time that I managed to doze off my surroundings would disrupt me. I had one too many of these interruptions and I decided that I had to go home. All throughout the next couple of days my flesh was warring with my spirit man. Should I continue to entertain this "friendship" knowing that it will only benefit my flesh? It did feel good to wake up to someone. I wouldn't mind being in his arms again. I can handle a purely physical relationship with him. Maybe I could just fornicate now and repent later. On the other hand my spirit was fighting back. ***"Don't be entangled with the yoke of bondage again."(Galatians 5:1)***

You can't keep going like this think of all you would be giving up. Do you really want to pay what it costs to test the waters? This is not right and you know it. If you sow to the flesh you are going to reap spiritual death. Have you come all this way to get sidetracked and fall now? You need to end this before it gets worse. Look at the state you are in. You are actually contemplating sin as an option.

This raging battle is what caused me to seek God for an answer that would stop my head from spinning. "God I know that I don't deserve to hear from you but please give me an answer. Please God." Still met with silence I make my way to my bus stop. I was relieved to see that my bus had arrived early. I boarded when a particularly eerie feeling overshadowed me. I chose to ignore it and sat down. After about 5 or ten minutes I looked at my cell phone and noticed that this bus was unusually early. It was only 8:11am and my bus wasn't due to leave the station until 8:20am.

Before I had boarded the bus I took note of the sign. The sign on the side read "Williamsville." So how come it's so early? A few more minutes pass and I take note of the sign scrolling inside of the bus. It too read "Williamsville" but as I kept watching the sign also read "Transit Rd." and "Transit Town Plaza." I am on the wrong bus.

How could I have gotten on the wrong bus? I take this route all the time. Well it does go to Transit Road. Maybe I could just ride until I get a little closer to my destination. Oh wait what if the right bus comes and I miss it? It was at that point that I decided to get off at the next stop.

So there I was cold and wet from the in climate weather. At least I wasn't due to work for another 45 minutes. Then the thought hit me like a ton of cement. I had given up my transfer (ticket to ride connecting bus for 45 cents or so) and it would now cost me more money to get on the correct bus.

I took some money out of my wallet and waited for what seemed like forever in the freezing rain. The right bus finally came and while riding God began to speak to me. "I let this happen to show you what you are headed for if you don't make the right decision. It is going to cost you so much more than you realize. You can only get but so far on the wrong path. It might look like the right way but you stay on this path and you are going to miss my promises."

> *Elijah came near to all the people and said, How long will you halt and limp between two opinions? If the Lord is God, follow Him! But if Baal, then follow him. And the people did not answer him a word.* 1 Kings 18:21

1 Kings 18:21 came to mind when I examined my situation a little further. A couple of my dear friends worded it this way; "Rita what do you want more? The will of God and the blessings that follow or your flesh to be satisfied temporarily?" The "wrong bus" would have only brought me into close proximity with my destination. I would have been like Moses in the wilderness, able to see the promised-land but made to live outside of it.

The enemy loves to keep you contemplating staying on the wrong path. His objective is to have you wavering between two opinions long enough to make you miss your appointed place of promise.

Don't miss your appointment! Do whatever it takes to get all that God has said is yours. For some of you this may mean beginning with a decision to commit your life to the Creator by submitting and following the Lord and Savior Jesus Christ. You have been sleeping for far too long. Don't you want to truly live? The steps to salvation are easy. According to Rom 10:9-10,

> *Because if you acknowledge and confess with your lips that Jesus is Lord and in your heart believe (adhere to, trust in, and rely on the truth) that God raised Him from the dead, you will be saved. For with the heart a person believes (adheres to, trusts in, and relies on Christ) and so is justified (declared*

righteous, acceptable to God), and with the mouth he confesses (declares openly and speaks out freely his faith) and confirms [his] salvation.

All that this scripture means is that if you believe with your heart and confess with your mouth that God raised Jesus from the dead and by doing this he paid for your freedom from sin and spiritual death that you will have eternal life with him in heaven when you pass from this life; Then your sins are forgiven and you are saved.

If you want to receive salvation but don't quite know what to say just read the statement below. You may want to read it a few times silently before you say it aloud, as to really connect with it and then read it aloud.

Jesus, I know that I have sinned and that I have no life without you. I recognize that God sent you to die and be raised from the dead for my salvation. I accept that when you died and rose from the dead you freed me from Satan's power. I know that I will not be perfect and acknowledge that I may make mistakes from time to time. I thank you for forgiving and saving me now and leading me in a plain path in Jesus' name. Amen.

Welcome to the Body of Christ! I recommend that you find a good Bible believing, Word of God proclaiming church. A church whose Doctrine states that Jesus is the way the truth and the life and that he will return for his spotless bride(The Church) one day. In making this commitment you have both acknowledged your need for God's guidance as well as taken a necessary step needed to redeem the time.

Just a few tips to help you in your new relationship with God: **Pray Daily—talk with God like you would talk to a loving parent or best friend.** He wants to hear from you. You can tell him about your day, ask him for peace, tell him you love him, ask him for help and instructions. Whatever you need God is there and He's listening.

Find a Bible to read and study from. Reading the Bible, perhaps the New international Version **(NIV)** or Amplified Version **(AMP)** is a great way to add strength to the foundation of your growing relationship with Christ. These versions of the Bible are very easy to understand they tend to offer an explanation to all of the difficult terms of the King James Version **(KJV).**

Find people who are already Christian. They can help build you up. There is strength in numbers. You are going to have questions that need answers. The Christians that you surround yourself with (if they have strong faith and conviction) will provide the boost you'll need to stay focused and on the right path.

Realize that you will make mistakes. Don't beat yourself up. God isn't waiting for you with a "lickin' stick" every time you mess up. This is not by any means permission to continue living a sinful and self-gratified lifestyle. It is simply a truth. We are all human and if we aren't careful we will give in to temptation or have a moment of weakness that leads us to sin. Know that you can come to God and ask for forgiveness.

If you are sincere with God He will be faithful and just to forgive you. As *1 John 1:9* states,

> If we [freely] admit that we have sinned and confess our sins, He is faithful and just (true to His own nature and promises) and will forgive our sins [dismiss our lawlessness] and [continuously] cleanse us from all unrighteousness [everything not in conformity to His will in purpose, thought, and action].

13

GET READY . . . 'CAUSE HERE COME THE OBSTACLES!

Satan's secret weapon is Distraction. If he can get you sidetracked enough to miss your divine appointment, then he knows that one less purpose will be fulfilled. Those who are affected by your decision to "Sleep on" can range in size from tens to tens of thousands.

There is one consistency throughout this illustrative thought, and that is in certain scenarios the main character yields to an undetected distraction. Another of Satan's objective is to use the things that we like, desire or lust after to create an obstacle. This obstacle is such that we turn off course and follow after that which entices us rather than continuing on in purpose.

Know that distractions will come. As long as you and I are breathing and walking on the face of the earth there will be road blocks that trip us up. You can't blame the devil for everything. If we are honest with ourselves, we know that there are things that we indulge in that keep us from staying the path. This is not necessarily sin. It could be talking on the phone until late knowing that you have a business meeting to attend in the morning. It could also be going to the movies instead of studying, drinking too much, or entertaining the wrong group of people.

No matter what the cause of this distraction, you must first learn to identify the distraction. You have to identify it before you can cut it off at the root. For example, a Gardener plants a small vegetable garden. The 3rd month in this process the Gardener notices that his tomatoes aren't in bloom. Does the Gardener then pull up the Garden or does he assess the land first?

Think of your life's destiny as a garden which you are left to tend. In this garden the "weeds" are choking the life out of your harvest. What are the weeds? I'm glad you asked but in truth it is you who holds the answer. You see, the WEEDS are **W**ays of **E**ntanglement or **E**ntrapment **D**esigned to **S**tagnate. Every weed has a root but in order to get to the root you must differentiate between the weeds and the fruit.

Every one of us is the "earth" that our destiny needs to flourish, and as with any other garden the earth is capable of producing weeds alongside of its harvest. So what's inside of your earth that is hindering your destiny? This question is the first step in assessing your garden and continuing on the path of redeeming the time. Pay attention to yourself. Some of the things that you least expect could very well be *WEEDS*.

I too, started a process of uncovering the *WEEDS* in my earth. While paying very close attention to the things that I liked, I realized that I was putting things in my earth that were good at the time but deadly in the long run.

For instance, I liked to drink on a social basis only. Having a Strawberry Daiquiri here and a Long Island there, until one day I found myself buying cases and bottles for my home enjoyment. Still not seeing the harm I continued to drink socially and at home. The number of drinks however, kept increasing and I kept insisting to myself that I was okay after all I was just having fun.

An unfortunate case of depression set in and I began to turn what was as "innocent" as social drinking into a coping mechanism. As a result, I spent years asking God to help me gain control, healing and deliverance. I liked to drink and thus I created an avenue that the devil and I could use to distract myself. I still know what drinks taste good and every time I get discouraged, upset, or tragedy strikes it is a possibility that I will be faced with the challenge to follow after the entanglement or to stay the course to destiny.

What is the root? Since every weed has a root you cannot afford to cut the weed from the surface and leave the root behind. The WEEDS that are after your destiny stem from some place. That place is how that weed survives. So what's feeding your WEEDS? The Root, simply put—the **R**eason **O**ur **O**bstacles **T**akeover.

In my case when I decided not to drink anymore, I was cutting down the weeds and leaving the root. Now you may be thinking, "How's that?

Deciding not to drink is a good enough decision by itself." True enough while abstaining from alcohol is a major step in living a sober life, it is not the all inclusive step needed to stay sober. In order to truly destroy this weed's stronghold I had to go after its root. My focus was now set on doing away with the very root that had attached itself to the seed of my destiny.

My ROOT was that I didn't like confrontation. I fled from it at the slightest appearance. I used alcohol to as a substitution for dealing with real hurt, doubt, fear, worry and anger.

So even though I had stated that I would no longer drink, I continually broke my vow, because I didn't know how or even want to confront and handle my emotions and adversities. In the words of a wise leader "You cannot change what you will not confront. Confrontation is the breeding grounds for growth."—Bishop Nathan S. Halton

We have to confront our hindrances and distractions head on in order to have a life filled with good fruit. The obstacles that arise can be overcome once we become aware of our areas of weakness and struggle and deal with them appropriately.

"Embrace this gift that we call time. Understand its value and cherish each moment more than the last."

14

REDEEMING THE TIME

In the introduction to this book I quoted **Romans 13:11(AMP)** which states,

> *Besides this you know what [a critical] hour this is,*
> *how it is high time now for you to wake up out of your sleep*
> *(rouse to reality). For salvation (final deliverance) is nearer*
> *to us now than when we first believed (adhered to, trusted*
> *in, and relied on Christ, the Messiah).*

It is only befitting that I make reference to this verse in this section of the book. Knowledge of the fact that time has been wasted is not going to change anything. It is time for you to rouse to reality. Stop hitting the snooze button and blaming everyone else for the life you are living. Today is not the last day of your life so there is still time to turn it around. Allow me to highlight a few points that I have shared throughout the book. I also want to share a few tools that I feel would benefit you as you journey toward successfully waking up on time.

There is an alarm that is internal we all have one and at different points in our life it begins to sound. Here is where we need to respond but how? Realize that the alarm can be set and reset but must never be ignored.

I asked you a question in chapter 8, Is your assignment begging you to wake up? Well is it? You see, the time for you to unlock change is now and here is the first key. **Stop, look and listen!** Hebrews 12:1-2

> *Wherefore seeing we also are compassed about with so*
> *great a cloud of witnesses, let us lay aside every weight, and the*

sin which doth so easily beset us, and let us run with patience the race that is set before us, Looking unto Jesus the author and finisher of our faith; who for the joy that was set before him endured the cross, despising the shame, and is set down at the right hand of the throne of God.

It is imperative that you stop giving in to sin and those bad habits. Start running toward your goals and promises. Take a look at what your life is like right now and assess it. Is this the life you've always wanted or the one you got stuck in? Examine every facet of your life in total honesty and then work to get rid of those habits and hung ups that are holding you back.

Listen to the soundtrack of your life. Does it sing to the tune of complacency and disappointment? Are you speaking complaint after complaint about how if you had only done this then that wouldn't have happened? Are you listening to temptation's lullaby? This bitter sweet song temptation sings only yields a temporary high and causes devastating lows. Don't flirt with temptation. No matter how alluring and enticing it may seem it leads to emptiness. You have to do something that is productive and demands your undivided attention.

This leads us to the second key. **Drop your excuses.** Let go of the 'I can't and it's not my fault' excuses. The excuses that you make today are the reason that you don't have the life you want. How long will you clutch the "comforter" of the current stagnate life while lying on the bed of bad decision? Change your mind's eye. Instead of seeing all the potential reasons that oppose the possible, retrain your mind to form every reason why you should and are going to complete the task. No excuse is worth sacrificing a joyful and fulfilled life. Start fresh right now. Every time you think you can't or aren't qualified or equipped enough, take away the negative words and replace them with *"I can do all things through Christ that strengtheneth me."(Philippians 4:13, KJV)* Starve your excuses with what God says and believes about you.

This brings us to our third key, **Have a plan!** There are steps that you need to take in order to see the joy-filled days that you long for. Whether it is in business, Church or at home with your family you need to have a plan of action. What course of action can you take right now to get the ball rolling in the right direction? Create a strategy for living in fullness. Start by praying and asking God what He wants to do with your life, family and business (*if applicable).* Give Him room to guide you as you write out the plan.

Your life plan is meaningless if you don't talk to your creator first. Next you will want to jot down a few attainable goals. These goals must be realistic. Don't sabotage yourself by writing dreams instead of goals. You must first meet your goals in order to reach your dreams. What good is saying "I'm going be a millionaire" if you don't first plan to save or invest. Give yourself at least a 6 month time frame to meet 2 goals off of your list. Make the goal list about 8 items long. Give yourself a 2 year time period to chart your progress completing 2 attainable goals every 6months.

After you have reached all 8 of your goals do a self evaluation. Did the goals that you set for yourself improve your life, family and business *(if applicable)*? Are you living your Dream or closer to it than you were? Is your family stronger and closer than ever? Is your business breaking records and yielding the results that it needs to in order to maintain an excellent standard? Does your ministry affect its surrounding community or city the way it should? All of these questions you can use to gauge the success of your plan. You should write them down and keep them close to your list.

This is not a New Year's Resolution so don't think that you can say it and then not keep your word. Make a covenant with yourself and God that you will put forth an effort to see these goals through. The trick is to set the most attainable goals that are within your power to complete but will take discipline to finish (i.e. save money, once a week going to an event with your family, setting up a business plan, getting your congregation the tools they need to be debt free). The goals you set are not punishments they are tickets to bettering your life.

Now that you've set realistic and attainable goals you will need the fourth key. **Learn when to say No!** Everybody has an opinion but not everyone's opinion is detrimental to your success. Saying no is the most powerful tool that you have against the popular opinion. People who are closest to you will sometimes try to convince you that what you believe or want to do is too big or too outlandish for it to materialize. It is at this point that you should say "No!" and like David you must realize that you "can't go with these" erroneous ideas of what you can and cannot do.

The thing that you have to remember is that, when you are considering doing something great or different than your norm it makes those around you nervous. After all, they've never seen you do this and therefore their opinion of the situation is that you can't. God created you and the criticisms of those around you don't hold a candle to the loving guidance that God gives. It does take work to see a dream come true and as long as you are willing to work towards it God will see to it that you are blessed to get there.

After you have learned to use your "No" effectively you will be well on your way to doing what it takes to fulfill your purpose. Our fifth key is that we must learn to **Value Time (a major component in setting the alarm).** What is your mindset as it relates to time? Do you feel that you have plenty of time to fulfill all your heart's desires? Are you nonchalant about the amount of time you spend doing pointless things? Do you find that you waste more time than you spend? or Do you spend too much time? We fail to realize that if we spend too much time on any one portion of our life, we run a great risk of leaving other equally as important areas in our lives unattended and neglected.

Deem your time as valuable. Respect time. Don't waste and abuse it. It flows one way and stops for no one. This moment is gone and the next moment is soon to pass. What you think about time depicts how you make use of it. You don't have time to hold useless conversations about who slept with whom last week. You don't have time to ignore your wife, husband, kids or fiancée. You don't have time to sit hoping for a better tomorrow. All you have is now.

Our sixth key is learning **The Art of Balancing.** Too often we stress over seemingly not having enough hours in the day. The truth is we don't need another 8 hours tacked on to our already jam-packed day. We need to manage the 24 hours better. I don't know a single person that hasn't said "I wish had more time." To me this is a sure fire sign that that particular individual did not plan their day.

I am fully aware that things don't always go according to plan. That doesn't mean that you shouldn't have one. A basic outline of what your day should look like is what I am referring to. If you have an outline in place and Johnny gets sick then your priority shifts to take care of little Johnny. Outside of emergency and unforeseeable occurrences your day should follow a plan.

Timeliness is not only necessary but is also an important factor in how smoothly our days run. You need to have a reputation for arriving early to appointments, interviews and to work. On time is late and 15 minutes early is on time. That is the Golden Rule of timeliness, cherish it and use it to replace the bad habit of showing up late. Being late and reckless with time is no longer acceptable.

Prioritize your life. Realize that not everything is a priority. Create a list of everything that is worth your time. This list should read; God, Family, Myself, Career, and Friends. Essentially, it is up to you how much quality time will be invested into each category. The amount of time spent is directly related to the growth and development of each aspect of your life. To maintain balance every column should be weighted on a scale from least to greatest amount of time allocated.

On average you have about 8 hours to spend after work (if employed full time). In those 8 hours you have to feed yourself and or family, unwind from the stresses of the day and prepare for the next day. Allot time for each item on your list. The times may vary from day to day and month to month but make sure you establish a minimum and maximum set of minutes for each component.

Portion control isn't just for meal time. Rationing out your time will enhance your overall wellbeing. Once you have it written it will be easy to establish a routine and order for your life. I want you to understand that if you aren't balanced as an individual nothing that you put your hands to will be balanced either.

> *[For being as he is] a man of two minds (hesitating, dubious, irresolute), [he is] unstable and unreliable and uncertain about everything [he thinks, feels, decides].* James 1:8

This scripture is definitely one that you should commit to memory. It is an essential component to waking up on time. You have to be sure that you are ready and unmovable in your mind. An unstable thought process yields an unstable life, family, business or church. This leads me to offer my next key.

The seventh key is to **Count up the cost.** What is it going to take in order for you to walk in abundant life? First, it takes a lot of focus. Your sights have to be set on the end result. Raising children, creating a strong bond between husband and wife or intended spouse, or leading a congregation or business requires that you maintain a clear view of what your goal is and the path to obtain it.

Secondly, you need to be consistent. Without consistency you will lose focus. Consistency is having the ability to maintain stability. You can't be on track today and off track tomorrow. You either want change bad enough to continue or you don't. It's just that simple.

Thirdly, you need determination. Determination is the glue that holds the other two principles together. You have to become impassioned enough to not let anything sidetrack you or hinder your progress. It is only when you have truly gained strength of mind that you will begin to push past road blocks and opposition.

You can't just sit back and have visions of grandeur and no plausible way of ever causing them to become reality. You know why so many of your dreams, visions and failed attempts at success happened? You didn't think the plan all the way through. You got excited over the idea of being happily married with children, having that Fortune 500 Company or leading that Mega Church.

You didn't count up the cost you simply dove in head first without so much as a clue on how to see it through to the end. When the first storm wind blew you tucked tailed and hauled butt out of dodge. Why? Because you underestimated the amount of effort it takes to build a company, family or congregation.

The eighth and final key is to learn to **Tithe your Time**. God lead me to tithe my time during the course of writing this book. I was in prayer and God laid it on my heart to give Him 3 consecutive days outside of my devotional time that would be spent just communing with Him. I don't ask God for anything materialistic in this time. I spend this intimate time in worship, reading The WORD and talking to God about what he sees and wants done in my life.

My life's priority is to be in the will of God. I believe that the principle of tithing when applied to our lives can be vital to the quality of life that we live. I challenge you to spend quality time with God. Build your spiritual relationship with God your father and watch your life grow more stable and full of joy.

You no longer have the option to oversleep. Your life is waiting for you to invest into it. You have keys to your future, instructions on how to set the alarm and all the reason in the world to wake up on time. Will you sleep through yet another alarm?

FINAL THOUGHTS

The night is far gone and the day is almost here. Let us then drop (fling away) the works and deeds of darkness and put on the [full] armor of light. **Romans 13:12(AMP)**

The alarm has sounded and with well rested eyes you peer into a day full of promise. You depart from your bed and prepare for the best days of your life. Ready to shed the garments of the night and enrobe yourself with the apparel of joy, you approach your day. Today is the day that you conquer your enemy. Release your slumbering state and discard the former mentality that held you captive in the chains of misery and discontentment.

Destiny awaits you my friend and success is extending her hand. Don't hesitate to shift directions and aim for the better half of your life. Time will outlast us all and that is why we must make the most of it. Your Family, Community, Business and YOU deserve to experience the wealth of life. Don't forget to set the alarm. Good Night!